D1452925

Angel Chatter

Heavenly Guidance and Earthly Practice to Connect with Angels

Christine Alexandria

Helios press

Copyright © 2017 by Christine Alexandria

Illustrations copyright © 2017 by Christine Alexandria except illustrations on pages xii, 22, 38, 52, 66, 80, 96, 110, 124, 138, 152, 168, 180, 194, 208 by Mere Stone

All rights reserved. No part of this book may be reproduced in any manner without the express written consent of the publisher, except in the case of brief excerpts in critical reviews or articles. All inquiries should be addressed to Skyhorse Publishing, 307 West 36th Street, 11th Floor, New York, NY 10018.

Helios Press books may be purchased in bulk at special discounts for sales promotion, corporate gifts, fund-raising, or educational purposes. Special editions can also be created to specifications. For details, contact the Special Sales Department, Skyhorse Publishing, 307 West 36th Street, 11th Floor, New York, NY 10018 or info@skyhorsepublishing.com.

Helios® and Helios Press® are registered trademarks of Skyhorse Publishing, Inc.®, a Delaware corporation.

Visit our website at www.skyhorsepublishing.com.

10 9 8 7 6 5 4 3 2 1

Library of Congress Cataloging-in-Publication Data is available on file.

Cover design by Jane Sheppard
Cover photo by iStockphoto

Print ISBN: 978-1-5107-2749-6
Ebook ISBN: 978-1-5107-2750-2

Printed in the United States of America

*This book is dedicated to all who wish to chat with the angels
in a more fluid, easy, and joy-filled manner throughout each and every day.*

Table of Contents

Introduction

Angels.

They are my buddies, my pals, my guides, my wing slappers. They have been with me my entire life helping to open doors, clear paths, and, when necessary, stop me from doing anything stupid (aka human). Who knew this could be an actual blessing? I certainly didn't, or at best, didn't acknowledge it. It wasn't until I started getting feedback from clients and students about how beneficial our sessions were that I thought, *perhaps*.

I've always been sensitive to how others are feeling. I knew when they were happy, sad, or excited just by thinking about them. I don't know how I knew; I just did. I distinctly remember playing with friends at the ripe ol' age of six when one of them asked how I "knew everything." In that moment, I realized that they didn't "know everything," and that this fact made me different; not in a way I liked. Within moments, I shut down.

At the age of six.

Sigh.

The sensitivity stayed with me, albeit not as strong. While I still felt the energy of others, I no longer shared. I knew their moods just by listening to the tones of their voices, no matter how hard they attempted to camouflage. I developed nervous twitches, for which I had medical tests done, but there was nothing medically wrong. I found great solace in ballet. It was solitary and I loved the movement and music, not to mention my teacher, La Nada. She helped me in ways beyond perfecting a *tour jeté*. She taught me that being unique was a grand and glorious thing, and planted the seeds that I was encouraged to grow many years later; seeds that now remind me to be me and not try to be like another—either through mimicking or the energies of jealousy and attempting to keep them in their spot. Neither serves well. It's why when I cheer you on, it is done with a full heart and much joy that is all directed outward. All deserve to be comfortable with themselves and share who they are with true aplomb. Thanks, La Nada.

I went to college and made friends. Some became roommates and we started to conquer the world as we joined the workforce. My roommates understood my knowings and didn't think it odd when I called to ask what was wrong. They accepted me for who I was/am and I felt safe. Sure, I dated, but nobody knew what I did—shoot, *I* didn't fully know, let alone understand! In fact, my husband likes to tease me that I did a bait and switch; that's how deeply hidden my blessing was. He didn't know about this until a good fifteen years after we were married! However, these great friends proudly cheered me on with phrases such as "It's about time!" when I finally "came out."

All this sensitivity continued to surround me. I still knew stuff. I would go to business functions with my husband and tell him who to avoid and who to attract. He listened. I could feel another's energy, and through that, their integrity. There is a word for this sensitivity: empath. Who knew? An empath is one who can sense energies from others and typically takes them on as their own mood. Unfortunately, if one isn't aware that the energy is a result of another source, the empath can become ill, depressed, or unsettled. At the very least, he or she can become withdrawn as it becomes too difficult to function out there. The energies are very real, as an empath absorbs them like a sponge. For example, some feel an earthquake building for days prior; feelings of shakiness (excuse the pun) take over their being.

Our pets are very much the same; not having been programmed to know what is acceptable or normal, they act as they feel. As an example, my dog, Gabi, knows when a thunderstorm is imminent even before the clouds darken the skies. She becomes needy, a true shadow to me, and tries to hide. Whether it's human or animal, it's all energy that is being felt. I'm lucky in the sense that these energies do not control my being to the point of becoming overwhelmed. While I certainly sense the unease, I've also learned how to disengage at varying levels. I know when it is me versus an outside source. Do I get warnings of catastrophic energies? At times, but this is luckily not a gift that is high on my list of gifts. It is for many empaths, and I feel for them; it can be a heavy load to carry, indeed.

I became a stay-at-home mom and loved it and all that it encompassed: nurse, cuddler, cook, chief bottle washer, mediator, chauffeur, book reader, and more. Unbeknownst to me, the angels began to creep in. Slowly, ever so slowly. I thought I was making this crap up and entertained the idea that, just perhaps, I was a bit psycho. Sure, I dabbled, went to readings, took classes, and even got trained in a few healing modalities, such as Reiki and Integrated Energy Therapy. I affectionately call this time "The Dunno Years." Why? Well, every time I took a class, my amazing husband would ask, "What are you going to do with this?"

"Dunno."

"When are you going to see clients?"

"Dunno."

"Are you going to teach?"

"Dunno."

And so on.

The angel-creeping intensified. I began reading magazines, seeing them everywhere I looked, and more. Perhaps it was just a passing fancy. The angels would laugh, hanging their heads in frustration at my thick-headedness, until the light finally dawned on Marble Head! Finally, and luckily for me, I had a reading where the reader called upon Archangel Ariel for guidance. Before I knew it, I yelled out, "Pinky!" My hands clasped over my mouth. Honestly, I don't remember a thing other than that from that reading. Oh, but what a thing.

My husband was traveling for business, so upon retiring to bed that night, I asked out loud, "Who are you?" (Yes, I was a bit confused.)

At least this time I was expecting her/it/the energy to enter. When she reentered the room, I squealed in delight, "It's you!" I now recognized her. You see, Ariel is my guardian angel, and we used to chat away the hours while I was a babe in the crib. As a child in the crib, her name, Ariel, was unfamiliar. However, since Ariel glows the color pink, a familiar color, I gave her the very appropriate name of Pinky.

Whew, maybe I wasn't psycho after all!

The Dunno Years quickly melded and morphed into the Sponge Years. The door was certainly opening and I thought, just maybe, that there was a reason I was so interested in this field. Maybe. I couldn't get enough. All that training? I added to it with crystal knowledge, more energy therapy training, soul coaching, and, well, you get the idea. I began to see clients with great results. Step by step, tools were added to the backpack of angelic arsenal that I would let marinate for *years*. As each tool was added, the angels were a constant. They were always there guiding me to find the right teacher (many were not the best of teachers, but I still learned a great deal from them). I began teaching a two-hour class here, a Reiki training there. In fact, on the morning of my first time teaching a Reiki class, the angels gave me a symbol that I still incorporate in my curriculum.

It was an interesting journey, to say the least, of how each one of these angels came forward to be the core of what has come to be known as "The Gang" (the winged and haloed version, of course). They began to chat with me as a collective unit. They actually still do this, but will separate themselves from the pack depending on each individual situation and what a client may need at that moment.

At first, my conversations with The Gang were very much trial and error. Who was who? How did I know it was them? How did Michael feel differently from Raphael? What was each predisposed to do? While I'm empathic and intuitive, and of course, I trust them, things still have to make sense in order for me to share with you, my clients, and customers. Seriously, if it doesn't make sense to me, how on earth can I share with others? Besides, I don't like giving out information in the form of a tool unless I've tried it myself and feel comfortable in its knowledge and effectiveness (and it certainly helps to know it's empowering). In essence, I'm their guinea pig.

Therefore, this book has truly been years in the making. Many times, it lay dormant. There were times it flowed like Shakespeare (okay, in my mind it was Shakespearean quality); at times fear took hold: who was I to share this? The angels retorted, who *wasn't* I? Everyone has a gift. Mine happens to be chatting with angels and sharing their messages in a mainstream sort of way that makes them more accessible, which, of course, they are.

As you move forward in the book, Michael, aka Big Mike, is the first angel. He is always the first angel I introduce. He is the protector, the warrior in the purest sense of the angelic realm, and I feel better knowing you've been exposed to him first. He will help you stay energetically protected as you delve deeper into each story, which will allow you to travel further down your spiritual path.

From Michael, we travel up the chakra system, starting with the earth star chakra and Archangel Sandalphon so you may remain grounded as you become more enlightened. Chakras are those energy portals within the human body and slightly outside the body that offer insights to our physical, mental, emotional, and spiritual well-being. I've encountered so many who are spiritual and yet find it so difficult to function in the here and now. Society has even come up with various terms for these folks: spacey, flighty, an airhead, airy faery, etc. You get the idea. One of my yearnings is to prove that we can all be spiritual, but in a very grounded manner. We can all live through that moment of *now*, living in the present to fully understand each situation more clearly versus getting drawn into its human drama.

Each of the angels in this book is my personal gang member. They are the core of all things Angel Chatter and their energy is in each product as it is conceived and created. Each angel is in existence and presented here for a specific purpose, as you will discover. They have offered more information regarding their angelic symbol, their mission, and more. They have even offered tools or homework, if you wish to call it that, to help deepen your knowledge of them while expanding and empowering you. As a collective unit, they help to keep you balanced, centered, living more from the essence of love versus the essence of ego, which is so easy to do as humans.

If studying the angels more intensely intrigues you, please contact me. My course, The Angel Chatter Intuitive Course, offers more information and indepth homework to a growing community of profound Chatterers across the globe. Some words and phrases may be new to you, and it is never my intention to make you feel less than fantastic, so I've provided a glossary of terms in the back of the book (see on p. 223). Enjoy the gift that the angels have offered and remember to listen for their whisperings.

—Christine

1

Archangel Michael (Big Mike)

Angel of Protection

"Dearest one, call on me and I'll be there to help protect you, guide you, and yes, even periodically wing slap you—just like any other loving big brother."

—Archangel Michael

Archangel Michael is the most widely recognized angel in the world. He is revered in many religions, such as Judaism, Christianity, and Islam. He is one of the four archangels mentioned in the Bible, both Old and New Testament. He is the patron saint of the police force in the United States. Yeah . . . he is that famous.

Archangel Michael is my, and hopefully soon to be your, go-to angel for in-your-face empowerment and protection. Think of Big Mike as the best big brother you have ever had or will have. Big brothers not only tease, but protect and stand up for you. Michael will gently pull your hair, push, prod, and kick you out of your comfort zone at times to get you to do what you really desire to do and be. He does all of this and more with great love and humor. In fact, the more you chat with Big Mike, the more you will begin to realize that angels *do* have a very *big* sense of humor! They use this humor to make headway in assisting you in your chosen life path, and Michael is no exception. He cracks me up on a daily basis. Seriously. Isn't it monotonous to be talked at? Isn't it rather bothersome to always have someone telling you what to do, versus suggesting you *could* do something else? Michael does just that, but if you are dragging your feet about being proactive in something, don't be surprised if and when he pushes, prods, or pulls the rug out from under you—all with the intention to wake you up and get you going on your desired path.

Big Mike? Yes, that is my personal nickname for him, and apparently, he rather likes it. It suits him; he *is* big, after all. This chosen nickname also offers a nod to his massive protective energy all wrapped up in lots of big feathers.

Michael always has your back; he may tease you, just like a big brother would, but will protect you if any others dare to intimidate or scare you. All you have to do ask. No matter if it is mundane or life threatening, he will be there in a nanosecond. Don't be surprised if he reaches out in unexpected and magical ways.

Zodiac Association

Michael is associated with the zodiac sign of Leo. Keeping in mind that his humor is legendary, when I asked him why, he said, "I have fabulous hair, darling one!" While lions are certainly one of the more majestic creatures that walk the planet, they own this majesty. They are more comfortable within their own skin. However, Michael will remind you, in gentle ways, of course, that it really isn't always all about you. It's okay to take a backseat once in a while to allow others to shine. On the flip side, if you are the one hiding, expect a push and roar from Michael to get you going again!

Michael's Name Defined

As all names have a meaning, Michael is no different. His name is translated to mean "who is as God." What a beautiful reminder that can easily apply to you. *You* are a true reflection of God/Goddess. A beautiful being filled with love, light, joy, immense grace, and a bit of quirkiness thrown in for good measure. As a reflection of this energy, you have the ability to do all you desire. You know, those dreams that can keep you up at night, those dreams that feel real and leave you breathless due to all the beauty and joy it gives to you. Those are the kind of insights that the angels can sneak in to remind you of who you are and what you are meant to be doing. Michael holds one of the keys to help open those doors for you. His question to you is, "Will you step through?"

> "You are extremely worthy of having my presence
> in every part of your life, no matter what!"

As you begin to accelerate upward on your spiritual path and reclaim your truest essence, lower energies will do their best to keep you stuck. Those nasty lower energies love nothing better than to keep all in a place of fear and immobility. You may have experienced feelings of indecision, unworthiness, inability to move forward, etc. Those kinds of emotions are most definitely linked to those nasty buggers. To help keep you in pristine energetic shape, please call on Michael prior to a luxurious mani-pedi, massage, energy treatment, haircut, or meditation. Through Michael's protective powers, you can fully relax and enjoy your spa treatment or meditation practice. It will become more profound. Why? Because Michael and his gang are there to protect you.

Likewise, if you are an energy worker, healer, massage therapist, etc., ask Michael and his legions to stand guard as you work. By calling on Michael prior to any client work, you not only protect yourself, but also your client. This is just one of the things that will set you apart from others; your clients will feel safer while with you. They will feel more confident and nurtured, and because of that, you shall be better able to assist them. This also holds true for any remote sessions you may conduct. If your schedule is quite busy, call upon him each morning to keep your space sacred and joyous.

This is why he is always the first angel I introduce to people. By being acquainted with Big Mike first, you begin to allow that protection and safety to become part of your normal way of life. This is not only a safety precaution, but an empowering tool.

Feel free to invite Archangel Michael into any space you frequent: work, a cafe, the gym, etc. All you are doing is simply offering protection and safety for all. No hidden agenda except allowing all to shine their own light brightly in complete safety.

Enough said. Call on him whenever you feel threatened. He will be there before you can finish your plea.

Angelic Encounter

Here's my story: It had been one crazy strand of a chaotic few weeks that actually spanned the entire spring season. It started with my dad having a massive heart attack on the "day the elephant danced," as he calls it. (It felt like an elephant was dancing on his chest.) Dad not only survived, but is now thriving. I happened to be visiting them during this adventure; I naturally extended my visit to help be the comic relief and do what I do best: distract and comfort.

Shortly after, we had three back-to-back expos scattered around the region. While we came home in between each one to restock and refuel, we became tired. My youngest child had elective surgery approximately one week after the last show. I trekked across the Chesapeake Bay (about a four-hour journey) to be with her. If you have children and they have ever been operated on, you know how I felt. *Stressed!* She came through it with flying colors and was released later that day. I then gathered our eldest child and we headed to visit her; another hour away. We stayed for the weekend, made yummy food, nurtured, visited, and tried to relax. A few days later, my eldest and I drove back to her home for a farmer's market run and quick visit with her and her boyfriend.

I then left their home and headed back to my parents' home (another four-hour trek) to retrieve my Yogi Dog, Gabi.

Tired yet? I was.

As I drove along, Michael popped in to remind me to have him surround the car.

Michael to my right,
Michael to my left,
Michael in front,
Michael behind,
Michael above,
Michael below,
Please protect me wherever I go.

Shades of things to come?

All was going smoothly; there was little traffic, and I was driving familiar terrain. Gertrude, my handy dandy GPS system, then told me to turn onto a road I was unfamiliar with. Since it had been a while since I traveled this particular route, I thought I had forgotten it and listened.

Ugh. The road quickly became barely a two-lane road with no berms/shoulder or dividing line. Oh, did I mention it was *very* curvy? By the time I realized that this was not where I wanted to be, I thought, *how bad could it get?* and trudged on.

How bad could it get? Silly question.

Did I mention it was curvy? I drove on, knuckles becoming white as my hands gripped the steering wheel.

I called on Big Mike, just to make sure he was around. I was getting scared, and knowing that he was around helped rest my mind—a little. I mean, I knew I was driving well, but those curves were not making me comfortable, and I was unsure how other drivers would handle them.

I drove below the speed limit, very unlike me, and saw yet another curve up ahead. Before I could slow down more, a *big* truck was headed directly for me. Okay it wasn't an eighteen-wheeler, but I couldn't see the driver because he or she was up that high. I pulled over as far as possible and drove partly on the grass. The truck still didn't pull more to their side and kept plowing ahead.

Rut roh.

Before I knew it, I was pressing hard on the horn. How my hand got there still befuddles me. It was as if a hand had gently pried my hand from the steering wheel, placed it on the horn, and pressed. Hard.

The truck then pulled more to their chosen side, slightly slowed down, and passed me. I tell you, I think I could have put my hand out the window and touched the truck as it passed. Yes, it was *that* close. I exhaled. Who knew I was holding my breath? I looked in the rearview mirror; the truck emitted no brake lights and simply kept moving forward. Heart racing, glowing with sweat, I continuing driving white-knuckled for the rest of that trek and practically kissed the ground when I arrived at my folks' home. It was beyond a nerve-racking experience and took me hours to calm down.

The next day after sharing this story with a friend, she promptly wrote back that Big Mike popped into her office immediately after reading my story and said, "Yep, I was there protecting her." He appeared to her as a flash of white light surrounded by electric blue.

Whew.

Thanks, Michael.

Michael's Light Temple

Michael's light temple is located at Banff, near Lake Louise in Canada. As with all light temples, don't go to these locales and expect to see a physical building, shrine, grotto, etc. dedicated to the angel or ascended master. These temples are energetic in nature. However, it is always an interesting bit of information to know. Do you feel a pull to this area? Do you live near it? These offer hints to a connection to this angel that you may not have been aware of.

Banff is located in Canada's first national park in Alberta and is a continuation of the Rocky Mountains. The pristine energies of the Banff area meld beautifully together to encapsulate the energy of Archangel Michael and pure magic. He is a fireball of energy, so having his temple located near a lake helps to soften his energy and make it easier to assimilate.

Michael's Symbol

As you have noticed, Michael's symbol looks like a sword, and this is with good reason. He is the commander in chief of the entire angelic realm; the consummate warrior. He is often illustrated, sculpted, and painted carrying a sword. After all, every warrior needs a sword for protection, right? Michael's sword is depicted in two ways. One is your typical sword made of high quality metal with sacred gems adorning the knuckle guard, ready for action and to protect you from all harm.

The other version of Michael's sword is seen as a blue flame. To offer a visual, think of a Bunsen burner from your science class days in high school or the Jedi's sword from Star Wars. Just as those visuals offer, Michael's sword glows a similar beautiful light cobalt blue. No matter the version of the sword, it can and does cut through caca with laser-like precision, leaving only pure-ness in its wake. Caca? You know, crap, the bad juju that can weigh you down.

Like any sword in the physical world, Michael's sword is a vital tool that can cut through the madness that surrounds the human race; it cuts through what can hold you back. Through the fear, the guilt, the woe-is-me-I'm-not-good-enough syndrome, and so on. His sword cuts through those energetic cords that are attached to you from others and can oftentimes drain you. (We'll go more into energy cord cutting on p. 143 to complete the ritual.) His sword also protects, thwarting lower energies from attaching to you by either deflecting them or decimating them if they dare come closer.

This kind of protective energy is so liberating that I've installed him perma-nently in our homes, cars, children's dorm rooms, and at expos. By doing so, our space becomes more sacred. People naturally feel protected while visiting. We can relax and simply be ourselves while in our castle, no matter where we currently call the castle. Isn't that one of the goals of life? To relax and simply be you in your own home? You can do it, too! The process is quite easy.

Archangel Michael's Seal of Protection

Sit quietly and comfortably.
Call on Archangel Michael.

Breathe in for four counts,
Hold for four counts,
Breathe out for four counts.

Continue breathing slowly as you feel his presence build within your room.
You may sense the room get more crowded and/or warmer.
You may even hear him enter!

No matter what you sense or don't sense,
Know that Michael is with you.

Breathe in for four counts,
Hold for four counts,
Breathe out for four counts.

Ask that he stand guard over your chosen space from this moment forward,
Until you no longer desire his presence.

Envision his feet going through the foundation of the building,
(It does not matter if you are living in a high rise or a chicken coop or
something in between),
He will continue to grow in stature,
And he will soar through the roof with his sword drawn high.

Breathe in for four counts,
Hold for four counts,
Breathe out for four counts.

From this moment forward, lower energies will either be destroyed if they
dare to enter,
Or go elsewhere,
In fear of Michael and his legion.

This leaves your home, office, car, or other sacred space.

Breathe in for four counts,
Hold for four counts,
Breathe out for four counts.

Give thanks.

Breathe in for four counts,
Hold for four counts,
Breathe out for four counts.

This shield is permanent.
You may even leave it intact if you move,
As a gift for future residents.

Breathe in for four counts,
Hold for four counts,
Breathe out for four counts.

I'm often asked which room I place Michael in. This is a great question! Honestly, it's up to you. If your home feels relatively safe and comfortable, you may anchor him in your most used room. On the other hand, if there is a room that perhaps feels a bit uncomfortable, anchor Michael there. Remember, the entire abode will be protected; this is just where you have asked him to be anchored. Bottom line? Don't fret if you think you've anchored him in the wrong place—he's got you covered!

Your space is now protected by Big Mike and his legion of angels. Of course, if you request that they stand down, they will do so immediately; after all, you are in control and have free will. You may also check in with him periodically to make sure all is well for your peace of mind. Having Michael standing guard over your space does not replace space clearing (see p. 13). What it does do, however, is prevent those heavier, darker, lower, or negative energies from entering. If you are super sensitive and attract those that have skipped over, this can also keep them at bay, which will offer more restorative sleep, clearer thinking, and allow you to live life fully present and not scattered. However, if crossing folks over is a passion of yours, you may establish "store hours," allowing for sleep and a specific time that you wish to help them.

Michael's Compass Direction

Most angels tend to align with a specific compass direction. This does not mean you must face that direction in order to chat with them. (That's just silly—can you imagine? "I'm about to get in a car accident, but must face the correct direction in order for Big Mike to help.") The direction is helpful if you feel a particular kinship to that angel and wish to petition them by setting up a specific spot in your home or office. For example, let's say you or a loved one is in the police force. As mentioned, Michael is the patron saint of the police force in this country, and you would like to have comfort knowing that he is protecting you or your loved one. You could set up a picture of you or your loved one in Michael's direction of your home or in that location of a room.

So, without further ado, Michael is associated with the compass direction of south. The southern hemisphere tends to be more sun-filled, which is another nod to his planetary association: the Sun. As the south is more sun-filled, it also tends to be warmer. Another nod to Michael, as heat is one of his signs that he is present with you. In fact, the more you chat with Michael, the warmer you tend to become naturally. Remember, I just mentioned that heat is one of his signs. This can happen with those just getting accustomed to his energies as well as the most seasoned "Chatterer." This extra power boost is his way of showing you that he is, indeed, with you. The heat encountered is akin to a prolonged hot flash for those that have undergone THE Change. Unlike a hot flash, however, his signature heat tends to start in the solar plexus area and radiates outward. Isn't it also ironic that his day of the week is *Sun*day? The angelic signs are ever-present, we just have to be more observant to be able to connect those dots!

If you wish to create an altar, you could also add a candle or crystal, a statue or angel medal. Anything that reminds you of Michael and his mission is perfect. If you have a loved one who is often put in harm's way (police, military, etc.), a photo of them placed on the altar is quite lovely and powerful. The location of an altar can be on top of your fireplace mantle, end table, or bookshelf. The location ideas are endless, really. Because you are focusing your energy and decorating with a specific intention, this spot will become more focused with energy and therefore sacred.

Michael's Chakra Association

Big Mike oversees the solar plexus chakra, the place of empowerment.

The solar plexus chakra is . . .
The place of divine power,
The place of comfort of self,
The place of safety in the here and now.

The solar plexus is the color of dazzling yellow and is located in your abdominal region, slightly above your naval. It offers glimpses of wisdom on how you view yourself and your own personal power. Your solar plexus chakra illuminates mental power, vitality, confidence, as well as intellectual activity, joy, and laughter. When the solar plexus chakra is in balance, you are simply being you; no hidden agenda. You feel confident, energized, strong, and able to conquer anything in your path or anything you put your mind to! (Let me know when you leap tall buildings in a single bound.)

When the solar plexus is out of alignment, you can become domineering, aggressive, or overly sensitive, and display self-deprecating tendencies. You may even find your posture is more humped, rounded shoulders, concave. It's as if you are pushing your power to the caboose of a train and letting your mind lead you around. This is not a great way to live, certainly, for when the mind leads, fear can easily sneak in and keep you up at night.

Think of a time when you were out socially and felt a bit uncomfortable. You most likely crossed your arms over your abdominal region. This is the location of your solar plexus chakra. Without realizing it, you were energetically attempting to protect yourself!

Can you see how Michael's area of expertise of empowerment is naturally attuned to the solar plexus? He is the protector, and his protection allows you to feel more secure, and that security can quickly help you become more empowered.

Most chakras attune themselves to musical notes. This is one of the reasons toning is often recommended through Tibetan bowls, crystal bowls, singing, etc. One can feel the energy of that note hitting each chakra, bringing it into a more balanced state of being. The solar plexus attunes to the musical note of E as you are so *E*mpowered.

Michael also oversees another chakra: the throat chakra.

The throat chakra is . . .
The place of divine communication,
The place of divine self-expression.

This chakra is a beautiful blue akin to blue sapphire. It sings to the musical note of G, as in Glorious wisdom that is shared every time you communicate, for you take your time and share from the heart.

When your throat chakra is in balance, you more freely express your desires, you are optimistic, spontaneous, and full of awe. Your voice is clear, unwavering, and strong. You don't hold back when expressing yourself. You express with great joy, wisdom, and love. It's not that you don't care what other people think—but you really don't care what other people think. You know that what you have to share has value and not everyone is part of your tribe so it's A-OK if everyone doesn't get it. You know that by speaking your truth, you are attracting your tribal members with greater ease.

Cool beans, right? I mean who doesn't desire to have more folks in their life that get them? I know I do, and I also know that if folks don't get me, it's cool, too. Remember, you simply can't please everyone!

When your throat chakra is off-kilter, you become shy, untruthful, intro-verted, and suspicious of the world around you. You can become snide and judgmental; although often this tends to be a defense mechanism of protection, it still isn't very becoming. Think of the class clown from school who would quickly make him or herself known by acting up. If you think about it, this wasn't the real person showing up. It was all a diversionary tactic, a facade. These folks are often the most sensitive to the energies around them and have found a variety of ways to isolate and protect themselves through humor, self-sabotage, and yes, even bullying. All things to consider before judging another as a total goof, the expert in the pity party, and even those who pick on and belittle others. Try to step back and look at the larger picture of the whys. (Why are they acting that way? What goes deeper?) Not saying you'll be able to fix them, but at least having an understanding can go a long way in how you act and react to these circumstances. This does not offer a Get Out of Jail Free Card to anyone, but does offer a better glimpse as to why folks make stupid, aka human, mistakes.

If the throat chakra is more closed, the proverbial and literal lump in the throat can exist. It can then manifest as laryngitis, strep throat, thyroid, and/or gum issues. Have you ever noticed the shaky voice while you speak or the shaky voice of another? This can be a clear indication of not feeling comfortable with the power and the ability to share with great value. Take a deep breath and start anew. With practice, the voice becomes strong and sure.

If the throat is overly open, nonstop chatter can be evident as a way to keep busy. One can become overly authoritative, which can include a raised voice. Can you think of a time when you or someone you knew started yelling and the situation quickly spun out of control? This is a combination of the throat and solar plexus at work. Feelings of disempowerment often lead to yelling or total silence. Trust me, nobody is really listening. They are actively thinking of ways to get out of there and away. When the *inside voice* is used, more listen.

A great way to clear the energies of your throat chakra is by singing! Who hasn't sung in the shower or belted one out while driving? I've been known to do just this much to humor my honey. Don't you feel more energized after doing so? Don't you feel more centered and alive? Try it more often. The more you sing, the better it gets and the easier it becomes to express your truest self.

When you combine Michael's chakras and missions together, you will have empowered communication. For example, a daily question in our home, and most likely yours is, "What's for dinner?" I'm blessed for many reasons, and one of them is that my husband loves to cook.

Oftentimes I respond with, "I don't care." However, I had no idea, but this response began to annoy him . . . a lot!

When he shared this with me using the retort, "Why can't you make up your mind," my finger waving came out.

"No, no, no." I explained that I really didn't care, or put another way, "I'm open to suggestions. So when I do state a preference, you best listen."

We haven't had that conversation since, and now he feels free to make suggestions!

Ready to feel more empowered? Time for an activity!

Angelic Activity: Clutter Clearing

Michael, as mentioned already, can assist in cutting through the crap. What better way to de-crap than to declutter the stuff in your home, car, and/or office! This monumental activity greatly assists the entire chakra system, not to mention creating a more sacred space for you. The purpose of decluttering is to allow more of what you desire to come to you. By creating *space,* you are signaling the universe that you are ready for more. Don't believe me? Think of a book shelf, any ol' bookshelf will do. It can only hold so many books, right? Once full, books begin to fall off, then are stacked on top of each other, which leaves it looking cramped and slightly cluttered, right? When the shelves are roomier, not only does it look more appealing, but you are signaling the universe that you are ready for more knowledge to enter.

Decluttering can be a big undertaking and one I address on a very regular basis, which helps keep things more in their chosen place versus piled up in a corner. I keep our home, our home; not a gathering place for stuff. While it may not be white-glove-worthy at all times, it is our sacred space and we treat it as such. That's not to say we don't get cluttered periodically! Who hasn't had at one time a stack of magazines, unworn clothes, or a junk drawer in their life? I'm no different; however, I do give things a run-through on a regular basis, and while I'm not decorating for another's approval, I frequently get comments that our home feels restorative, peaceful, and loving.

With that in mind, it's time to clear out the truly unwanted, unused, and undesirable stuff. Here's a bit of clutter advice:

Love it,
Use it,
or Lose it!

Great words to live by. In other words, if you don't love it or use it, it's time to *lose it*! Donate, give, or throw out; it doesn't matter. What matters is that you clear the way for more of you to jump on in and join the party. When that clutter begins to diminish, you are energetically inviting what you desire to come in because now there is room (think of that bookshelf) and you have more energy. I've lost track of how many clients have contacted me after their clutter-clearing adventure with reports back how clear things are and they can't believe how much more energy they have. And the best part? Opportunities are being presented to them! Chat with Michael to cut through the web of clutter. He can and will gladly help illuminate the first layer that will be relatively easy to get rid of. Once accomplished, each space feels cleaner and clearer. Notice I said layer; I always find it funny that once done, and thinking it's now perfect, I go back to find more stuff to get rid of a week or so later! Another layer reveals itself and is ready to go bye-bye.

Here are some ideas of where your unwanted goodies can go:

★ Unused canned goods? Donate to your local food pantry.

★ Clothes? There are loads of places to donate; many communities have bins in public places for donations, or you can consign them.

★ Books? Drop them at your local library.

★ Decor? Perhaps consign. Not only do you clear out, but you could also get some money in exchange!

★ Furniture? Sell or donate! Habitat for Humanity, Big Brothers Big Sisters, or simply put *donate furniture* in your computer's search engine. You may easily find a local charity.

Before you know it, you'll wonder why you ever had most of what you got rid of while feeling lighter, happier, and more empowered.

Michael's Healing Crystals

One of Michael's favorite crystals is lapis lazuli. Lapis lazuli greatly helps with communication—true communication. Think about it; when one communicates more clearly, they speak the truth from the energy of love, not fear. It's the easiest sounding thing to do, and yet can be the most difficult. Speaking from love means no finger pointing, no raised voices, no fear, no angst. It's contemplative, sincere, and while it may share some difficult emotions, it is never done in the essence of getting even, lashing out, or whining. Lapis lazuli is also known to assist in alleviating stress, which can open doors to inner peace. It is great for business situations because it helps better judgments to be made. It is known to initiate creative ideas (which can include solutions) for all situations. My honey discovered it years ago and is rarely without a small stone in his pocket, no matter where he is. This from a corporate executive! Lapis lazuli can easily be found in raw form as well as in jewelry settings and carvings.

Angelic Aromatherapy

Here are some favorite scents I associate with Michael and why:

Hyssop: offers protection and consecration of ritual objects. Its resonation with Michael is easy to see: protection of self and objects.

Anise Star: used during consecration and purification rituals. Use to purify an area or when dedicating/consecrating an article of high importance. Add a drop or two on objects if you wish to make an altar with Michael in mind.

Dragon's Blood: very fiery indeed, and talk about its great protective energies! Dragon's blood is derived from the bright red pigment from certain plants in the succulent family.

Clove: very warming and comforting; two of the attributes Michael offers when near.

All of Michael's scents can be used in the form of candles, sacred misters, and/or roll-ons. Think of candles as a space definer, helping you to protect the space while calling in Michael's energy. Lastly, the roll-ons are directly applied onto your skin, offering subtle shifts within to offer the knowledge that you are protected as you go about your day.

Michael's Askfirmations

Why is it so easy for me to be comfortable in my power?
Why is it so easy for me to connect with Archangel Michael?
Why am I so protected?

Michael Fun Fact

Did you know Michael's tears formed the realm known as the cherubim? Cherubim are often depicted as lions or bulls, winged angelic beings. They are frequently found as statues guarding buildings. Yet another nod to Michael: they are protecting! You may now be thinking, those don't sound like the cherubim I'm familiar with, those adorable child-like angels. They're not; those cubby cuties are called Putti.

Guided Meditation with Archangel Michael

Sit facing south.

Inhale for four counts,
Hold for four counts,
Exhale for four counts.

Call upon Archangel Michael.

Inhale for four counts,
Hold for four counts,
Exhale for four counts.

Michael enters your space.

Inhale for four counts,
Hold for four counts,
Exhale for four counts.

His energy and presence is huge,
And yet very comforting and reassuring.

Inhale for four counts,
Hold for four counts,
Exhale for four counts.

You may feel your body reacting to his presence and get warmer.

Inhale for four counts,
Hold for four counts,
Exhale for four counts.

Your heart slows to a more relaxed pace in his presence.

Inhale for four counts,
Hold for four counts,
Exhale for four counts.

You are comforted.

Inhale for four counts,
Hold for four counts,
Exhale for four counts.

As Michael enters the room,
You remember,
He is the best big brother in the world.

Inhale for four counts,
Hold for four counts,
Exhale for four counts.

He approaches you.

Inhale for four counts,
Hold for four counts,
Exhale for four counts.

He stands before you, smiling his mischievous grin.
His eyes sparkle.
A gentle breeze enters your room to reaffirm his presence.

Inhale for four counts,
Hold for four counts,
Exhale for four counts.

He takes your hands in his.

Inhale for four counts,
Hold for four counts,
Exhale for four counts.

He reminds you of your greatness.

Inhale for four counts,
Hold for four counts,
Exhale for four counts.

He reminds you of your power.

Inhale for four counts,
Hold for four counts,
Exhale for four counts.

He reminds you that all you need to do is ask for his assistance.

Inhale for four counts,
Hold for four counts,
Exhale for four counts.

He chuckles and lifts your chin with his hand.

Inhale for four counts,
Hold for four counts,
Exhale for four counts.

You are a child of the universe and deserve all you desire.

Inhale for four counts,
Hold for four counts,
Exhale for four counts.

His hand returns to his side.
He continues to hold both of your hands in his one.

Inhale for four counts,
Hold for four counts,
Exhale for four counts.

His energy begins to gently fade, leaving you with the knowledge that he is,
Always with you.

Inhale for four counts,
Hold for four counts,
Exhale for four counts.

Repeat.

Inhale for four counts,
Hold for four counts,
Exhale for four counts.

As you count backward from ten to one,
You become more alert.

Inhale for four counts,
Hold for four counts,
Exhale for four counts.

You are aware of the sounds in your space,
The furnishings in your room,
Your breathing.

Inhale for four counts,
Hold for four counts,
Exhale for four counts.

You gently move your fingers and toes.
You breathe in deeply.
Exhale loudly.

Inhale for four counts,
Hold for four counts,
Exhale for four counts.

Welcome back to the present called life.

2
Archangel Sandalphon (Sandy)

Angel of Grounding

"Be ever-present throughout your day. By so doing, you can embrace the beauty that surrounds you."

—Archangel Sandalphon

Archangel Sandalphon is reported to have been the prophet Elijah. He walked the earth in the ninth century BC and is credited with being a wonder-worker in northern Israel by defending the works of Yahweh.

Did you notice that Sandalphon's name ends differently than most angels? Here's why: whenever you see an angel's name ending in "-on" it signifies that angel's existence actually began as a human, who became a prophet, who turned into an angel upon their death. This is obviously very different than pure angelic energy, which would have his name ending in "-ael" or "-iel." Bet you didn't know that, now, did you?

Whenever I feel off-kilter, a bit ungrounded, or even overwhelmed, I call upon Archangel Sandalphon. What a great angel to help me put things in perspective, get my feet firmly planted in terra firma, feel fully present, grounded, and completely me. In other words, I get back in my body. Have you ever had one of those days when you are on autopilot and barely have time to give thanks that breathing is a natural phenomenon? Me too. Those are the perfect days to chat with Sandalphon. He can and will help you address one task at a time, allowing you to be fully present and complete tasks quicker than if you were multitasking.

He can also assist when you are feeling challenged by someone; especially if that someone is respected or considered an authority figure. Think about it, when you feel like fingers are pointing at you, you're being scolded, or worse, you get that fight-or-flight response. Sandalphon won't help you with fight-or-flight, but what he will do is be present with you to help you stay present. He can and does help you stand your ground, so to speak; standing in truth and purity. This is not a form of protection in the literal sense, but rather empowering you to not back down and become submissive. By calling on Sandalphon, you will feel more rooted and can begin to share your reasoning with greater clarity. This is especially powerful when you combine his energy with Michael's.

Sandy not only helps you feel more present, but is very helpful in acknowledging and helping get rid of the stresses that can come with over-dependence. We all can become over dependent on someone or something. Who hasn't felt their life end when a spouse or parent or child or pet skipped to the other side? Or having any relationship end, no matter how beneficial it ultimately is? Unfortunately, we often don't realize how much of a role that person or pet played in our life until it is too late. Sandalphon can help you have stronger relationships because you are staying present and can better embrace each person's own unique energy while enjoying life more fully.

Zodiac Association

Sandalphon's zodiac connection aligns with Gemini. Geminis are twins, correct? So why would Sandalphon be associated with this sign? He is the twin of Metatron, as you will soon learn. Twins help to create balance. Twins help to complete. Twins help to *be*. With the duo personality traits that Geminis exhibit, Sandalphon will remind you that you are *all* of those traits. No need to switch on or off. Simply be you. The world will become a much easier place to live when one isn't switching gears to appease the masses.

Sandalphon's Name Defined

Sandalphon's name means "co-brother." His angelic twin is Metatron (notice the "-on" ending in Metatron's name, as well) who resides over the soul star chakra which is located approximately six inches above your head. (More on Metatron on p. 153.) While they are not twins in the literal sense, they are comrades helping to bring balance and beauty with heavenly infusions on earth. When their energy is joined, it is very balanced, which is great if you do any kind of spiritual work. You stay grounded while chatting with the angels! When their energy is fused, it collides, joins, and merges within your heart, helping you to stay grounded, expansive, and live through the strongest essence of love. It's why I call them the Dynamic Duo.

Angelic Encounter

Sandalphon is such a natural part of my day, it's hard to remember when he wasn't hanging around me. So, I asked him to remind me of a time when he and I shared a moment or two. Here is our story: Years ago, when we were still vacationing on our island, I had taught Reiki to a small group of folks. One of my students was a local going back generations, and he strongly suggested I apply for a business license. This made sense, and wanting to do things by the book, I applied at our local government office.

Most business licenses go for about $15. They charged me $1,500. Yes, that is not a typo.

That was the first clue that they weren't going to grant me my license.

One year later, still not giving me the license, a few locals approached me and strongly suggested that I pull my business application to get a refund. Something unheard of. This was when I put my foot down and refused. Somebody had to throw the feather gauntlet down, after all! I refused and told them that I would follow through, and thanked them kindly.

Second clue.

The powers that be decided to have a town hearing—about me!

Seriously?

Me?

It was very uncomfortable for me to not only speak before the town council, but to know that most of the town were not in favor. Some had gone to my website and saw I chatted with angels.

This beautiful little old lady gets up to the microphone and said that only God can tell you who your guardian angel is, and anyone else is working with the devil!

Oh boy.

Third clue.

I stood tall. My neighbor came to support me, as my family could not physically be there. I spoke eloquently, or tried to. I shared. I looked each one on the council in the eye and smiled.

I was present.

One council member compared me to a phragmite: an invasive marsh plant. He stated we had enough weeds on the island—while looking directly at me.

I was turned down. What a surprise, right?

Upon walking out, my student informed me that the little old lady was his aunt who had no computer. She was told what to say!

Was I mad? Honestly, no. I was incredibly mystified that fear could and obviously did run so deep. Sandalphon kept me ever-present throughout the ordeal. I went home and shared a glass of wine with my neighbor.

The angels, however, had the last word. The very next day, it hailed—in the middle of the summer!

Who says angels don't have a sense of humor?

Sandalphon's Light Temple

Sandalphon's Light Temple is located in the mountains of Andalusia. This beautiful mountain range is in southern Spain. Like Michael's light temple, I have yet to visit this area, but feel a longing to go. Many members of my family have been to Spain and it sounds magical.

Sandalphon's Symbol

Look at Sandalphon's symbol. Does it remind you of anything? It reminds me of a tree with its roots showing. Which is perfect, since Sandalphon's chakra is in the earth (metaphorically, of course). The symbol starts high above your physical body, just as an idea does. It shoots downward, allowing roots to take hold and become the mightiest of trees. You are a metaphor of the tree, sending deep roots into the soil so you may stand tall, strong, bendable with the wind, but not breakable. Become the tree, reaching deep down while reaching for the stars. Do this type of meditation daily and you will quickly become more present with life, enjoying little moments, and noticing the opportunities as they are presented.

Sandalphon's Compass Direction

Sandalphon has no known compass direction, so I chatted with him about why and his response was, "There is no need for me to be located or associated with one specific compass direction. Like my brother, Metatron, we are everywhere. We are all and yet nothing. We are everywhere to help you plant your seeds of desire in the proper place so they may grow."

There ya go.

Sandalphon's Chakra Association

Sandalphon's chakra affiliation is the earth star chakra. The earth star is located approximately six inches below your feet, and its color resonance is a deep, rich brown. Think of the most fertile soil to give you a visual idea of the richness of the color. The soil has all the correct elements to allow seeds to germinate and roots to grow and become established with ease. It has the perfect balance to retain water and allow the excess to flow elsewhere. What a beautiful place to not only be grounded, but to allow all of your brilliant and heartfelt ideas to take root and blossom, enabling you to soar!

With the proper nurturing, those mere seeds can grow into beautiful metaphors for your very life. Connect with your earth star chakra by feeling the energetic roots of your soul sending out tendrils into the earth. These tendrils, while small, are mighty and will quickly grow into strong and sturdy roots that will enable you to be grounded in the here and now. When you are actively working with your earth star chakra, you walk upon the earth with greater respect of not only Gaia, but of self, and feel your entire being elongate as it reaches for the heavens.

Think of it this way: all ideas start as a concept or thought. As you dwell upon an idea, it either begins to feel yummy or not. The not so yummy ideas are simply being presented, but not necessarily meant to be acted upon and nurtured at this time, or any time, by you. However, if the idea continues to intrigue you, I suggest keeping an idea journal. It is a place to jot down projects that you wish to perhaps act upon at a later date. By writing down these ideas, you not only keep things in one spot, but by releasing your thoughts to paper, you free your mind to focus on what is calling you more strongly. If you are highly creative, segregate your ideas into categories.

How to know if an idea is viable for you? Place your hands over your heart. Your heart is the birthplace of your soul and will never lead you astray. Close your eyes. Relax into the cadence of your breath and heartbeat. Sit quietly for a minimum of three minutes, just being. Think of your idea; does it settle in and expand? Or does it seem to float away? Therein lies your answer—whether it is a good idea to act upon, one for the idea journal, or one for someone else to take over. You can use the same exercise when investigating a new job, client, employee, mate, etc.

By being present, you recognize an opportunity when it is presented. You are aware of life around you: the beauty, the sounds, the textures, the aromas. One of the main purposes of the earth star chakra is to keep you fully grounded in the here and now while illuminating opportunities so you may manifest your heavenly aspirations. It greatly connects you to the magnetic force of the earth itself, helping to align and ground all of your bodies into one. Remember, being grounded does not mean stuck. When one is grounded, they become more present with life and are able to experience and recognize every circumstance for what it is.

If one has a balanced earth star chakra, they are present and able to manifest their spiritual desires more easily into the physical. They can see the big picture, have more peace of mind, and are generally more secure. If one has a more imbalanced earth star chakra, they may experience vertigo, circulatory issues, eating disorders (not feeling worthy of aligning all bodies), and lower body physical issues, such as ankles, etc.

Since Sandalphon's chakra is the earth star, is it any wonder that he is in charge of the world and humanity at large? Helping all to ascend on their personal trek and timeline. Helping all to become their truest essence and realize their divine greatness. There is never a rush to get there, as all is, indeed, divine timing.

Sandalphon is much more than just anchoring and planting inspirational seeds and keeping you present. He aids greatly in your physical vitality. So, on those days where nothing is going right and you feel quite lethargic, chat with him and he will be sure to suggest a multitude of activities to get your prana going! Then, take a walk on the wild side with nature. Do you not relax when sitting under a tree? Does stress not melt off of you when you spend time outdoors? Don't trees naturally heal us by giving off oxygen—the very thing that humans need to survive? Don't folks flock by the thousands annually to the mountains and shore with the sole purpose of relaxing? Nature heals in all its beauty.

Sandalphon is also incredibly instrumental in helping to see to the *root* of any situation. What caused them/me to act in this way? What is really going on here—the motivator? Sandalphon encourages you to take that proverbial step back to see the larger picture. Not sure how? Here's another tip from him: imagine you are attending a play at the theatre or watching a movie. It is engaging and you can foretell the actions of the characters. You see how and why they act the way they do without getting caught up in the drama itself. This process allows a better understanding of human nature, which of course includes you. Now, you can take any scenario in your life and turn it into a play using the same practice. As an example, you understand that sometimes people act out because they feel unloved, unrecognized, or unnoticed. When one understands the actions of another, life becomes less judgmental and egocentric. One can appreciate each learning adventure with a bit more ease, grace, and love toward all. When one begins to better understand the self, life's mysteries begin to unravel. One of those mysteries is the realization that all who are human, do human. All simply wish to be loved, including you.

Angelic Activity

Here's a beautiful exercise to help balance, align, and center you—with the assistance of Sandalphon, of course. This pose not only grounds your energies, but aligns your left and right meridians.

- ★ Sit in a chair.
- ★ Firmly place feet flat on the ground.
- ★ Crisscross your arms.
- ★ Place hands on knees with right hand on left knee and left hand on right knee; it doesn't matter which is on top. (Stop overthinking!)
- ★ Sit as straight as possible.
- ★ Breathe slowly and maintain pose as long as necessary.

Sandalphon's Healing Crystals

Sandalphon's crystal choice is a brown tourmaline and fulgurite. Brown tourmaline illuminates your deepest desires while grounding and cementing them into a physical manifestation. It offers deep grounding of self while offering profound self-acceptance that enables you to shine for the universe to see the real you. It is an ideal stone for self-healing and aids in finding emotional strength and self-acceptance. Brown tourmaline inspires courage and persistence. It calms and soothes, grounding and stabilizing the inner self.

Sandalphon's second crystal choice, fulgurite, is formed when lightning strikes, so is often referred to as petrified lightning. In fact, *fulgurite* is a Latin word for lightning. Each flash of lightning releases an average energy of 1 billion joules (unit of energy)! The lightning vaporizes the sand to make amorphous glass. Because lightning is instrumental in fulgurite's birthing, it is a highly sought after crystal for manifestation. Think about it, high voltage lightning creates a crystal; this can only yield a high-paced manifestation! The clear tube created by the lighting acts as a direct conduit for the energy of the divine mind to move into manifestation within physical reality. As the ambassador of prayer, Sandalphon helps lift your loving prayers to the universe with great ease and gets them answered. You can use a piece of fulgurite, if guided, as a megaphone of sorts to announce your desires more clearly. The key to having any prayer answered is stillness and the willingness to know that all prayers are being answered. Remember, you may get answers in a form you least expect. It is within that stillness that you shall receive them all.

Angelic Aromatherapy

Cedarwood: not only acts as an insect repellant, but also aids in respiratory and urinary complications.

Oakmoss: acts as a restorative. Don't you feel rejuvenated when you venture outside?

Sandalwood: how could it not align with Sandalphon? Seriously, this scent is known for aiding in mental clarity and memory boosting, and is even considered an aphrodisiac.

Sandalwood's earthly scent offers vitality while bringing spirituality to everyday living adventure. Try rubbing it on the soles of your feet to enhance its benefits. This practice is especially beneficial when done after a hot shower or bath, which opens your pores, allowing the essence and energy of the oil to travel with greater ease throughout your body. I do not recommend rubbing sandalwood on just prior to bedtime. Due to its energizing benefits, it could make you restless and sleep elusive.

Sandalwood oil is also extremely beneficial as a natural pesticide (it is known to repel ants) and aids in reducing skin inflammation. It acts as an immune booster, but also aids in the reduction of scars and soothing an irritated digestive tract. You see, it can be used for so many practices, every house ought to have some! Of course, sandalwood's benefits also align with Sandalphon's: immunity booster and good for health and digestion.

Sandalphon's Askfirmations

Why is it so easy for me to be ever-present with life?

Why is it so easy for me to ground my desires in the here and now?

Why is it so easy for me to be balanced?

Sandalphon Fun Fact

Sandalphon oversees all unborn children and helps determine the gender of each child born.

Guided Meditation with Archangel Sandalphon

Breathe in,
Hold for four counts,
Breathe out.

Call upon Archangel Sandalphon.

Breathe in,
Hold for four counts,
Breathe out.

Your eyes soften,
Your breath deepens,
Your body relaxes.

Breathe in,
Hold for four counts,
Breathe out.

As Archangel Sandalphon enters the room,
You feel a sense of peace,
Calm.
Groundedness, as if roots are extending from your body into the earth.

Breathe in,
Hold for four counts,
Breathe out.

Feel those roots become stronger as they dig deeper,
They are pulling the richness of the earth into your very being.

Breathe in,
Hold for four counts,
Breathe out.

As each root travels the globe,
It brings back to you what is needed for your,
Mind,
Body,
And soul.

Breathe in,
Hold for four counts,
Breathe out.

It brings back with it much needed information,
And energy,
To help fuel you as you walk your path.

Breathe in,
Hold for four counts,
Breathe out.

Allow your body to absorb and retain all that is needed.
Feel that energy flow upward into your physical body,
And permeate deep into your crystalline levels.

Breathe in,
Hold for four counts,
Breathe out.

As you continue breathing,
Sandalphon presents to you a crystal:
A brown tourmaline.

Breathe in,
Hold for four counts,
Breathe out.

This crystal holds within it energy of the best fertile soil,
The perfect combination to assist you to plant your seeds of desire,
So they may germinate, grow, and blossom while you remain present.

Breathe in,
Hold for four counts,
Breathe out.

Receive this crystal with the knowledge that its energies will go deep,
As you hold it close to your heart.

Breathe in,
Hold for four counts,
Breathe out.

Repeat.

Breathe in,
Hold for four counts,
Breathe out.

Sandalphon now asks that you look into his eyes.
They are beautiful,
Endless,
Wise,
Pure.

Breathe in,
Hold for four counts,
Breathe out.

Those eyes communicate to you,
All that you need to know,
In order to be more present with life.

Breathe in,
Hold for four counts,
Breathe out.

Sandalphon tells you how magnificent you are.
He reminds you that by being present in life,
You enjoy life to the fullest.

Breathe in,
Hold for four counts,
Breathe out.

This meeting is coming to an end,
But you know you may reconnect with Sandalphon,
Whenever you wish.

Breathe in,
Hold for four counts,
Breathe out.

As the energy becomes brighter, you become more present,
With now.

Breathe in,
Hold for four counts,
Breathe out.

The noises,
The textures,
The scents,
That surround you.

Breathe in,
Hold for four counts,
Breathe out.

Slowly open your eyes to a fresh new world.

Breathe in,
Hold for four counts,
Breathe out.

Smile and know life begins anew now.

Breathe in,
Hold for four counts,
Breathe out.

3

Archangel Uriel

Angel of Safety

"You are a brilliant soul that the universe needs to see.
You are safe to be you."

—Archangel Uriel

Uriel deals with the basics.

Safety is so basic, but such a big deal in being human. In the angelic world, don't confuse the words safety and protection. As you now know, Michael deals with protecting you, keeping you from harm. Uriel is quite different. He helps you feel safe to be you. How often have you done something, anything, in order to make another person happy? How many stories have you heard that the adult child went into the family business, but had no love for it and looked forward to retirement so they could then do what they most desired?

To put it in a larger context, if you are not living life to the fullest on your terms, there are indeed parts of you still hiding. As I shared in the first chapter, I called myself psycho for many years; hardly empowering. In fact, one could make a very strong argument that I was doing a great job at hiding and playing a game of making others happy at the expense of my own happiness. I allowed this to happen, so there is nobody to blame but myself.

Drat.

Uriel is less in your face than Michael. He opens doors for you to step through only when you are ready. There is no hair-pulling or prodding when it comes to Uriel. He will gently hold you in a safe cocoon of angels' wings until you desire to break free and be true to yourself and your dreams.

A universal symbol of Archangel Uriel is an open hand holding a flame. This represents God's truth, or the universal truth. Ironically, this was the logo for my previous business, InnerBalance; two hands uplifted holding a lotus flower that contained a flame. The angels have been speaking to me and through me for years, without my consciously realizing it!

Uriel's twin is Archangel Auriel. She oversees our angelic star chakra. Is it any wonder that Uriel is also known for helping us with our life path? Truly another fantastic duo. Auriel will assist in illuminating your chosen path, while Uriel can assist in the safety and security that you are the perfect person to go after your dream and achieve it.

Uriel is your go-to angel when you wish inertia to be removed to jump-start any area of your life. Diet? He's your guy. Career? Ditto. Romance and allowing true love to enter? Gotcha covered. He strengthens your ability to listen to the wisdom of your body, and infuses divine safety and drive, enabling you to go after what is desired with the utmost integrity.

One of Uriel's specialties is helping you achieve spiritual devotion through selfless service to others. Think of Mahatma Gandhi and Mother Teresa. They gave of self throughout their entire adult lives and beyond. Joan of Arc is another example, selflessly leading France to victory and pushing away true love for the service of God. Not destined to be a martyr or saint? Not to worry. Uriel can assist even us mere mortals in enlightening our personal lives to bring a bit more sunshine to another. Remember, a sincere smile can do more than an empty hug.

Are you a student of the law of attraction and the art of manifesting? You've been working with Uriel without realizing it. He teaches mastery of the material world. In other words, how to manifest exactly what you truly desire versus what you think you desire or need. If ever you are not sure, chat with him. He'll be sure to point out those retail therapy trips are really mindless fodder and you'd be better off staying at home or engaging in an activity that brings long-term joy to your world.

Zodiac Association

Uriel aligns with the zodiac sign of the goat, Capricorn. Goats can be stubborn, true, but goats know who they are and don't try to be anything but a goat. This is a true nod to Uriel, the angel of safety. He ever reminds you that you are safe to be you! Be headstrong in your beliefs, but allow other points of view to enter. Who knows, you may just learn a thing or two!

Uriel's Name Defined

Uriel's name means "Fire of God" or "God is My Light." Just another hint at how so many things are connected. Another way to interpret this meaning is that you are light, and as a child of God/Goddess, why wouldn't you be? When you are ready to shine, Uriel is right by your side helping to flip all those switches to on. He helps you shine your inner light and feel safe to do so. This allows the world to revel in your beauty, inner and outer.

Angelic Encounter

My adult life is in complete union with Uriel. Coming out and sharing that I am an angel intuitive, as you now know, was a very big deal in my world. Each time I launch a new product, Uriel is by my side. Each time I speak at a show, Uriel is right there. Each time I go outside my comfort zone with a new opportunity, Uriel is right there, too.

It became apparent as recently as last night. We were at a friend's store to celebrate their wedding anniversary, which happens to fall on July 4th, Independence Day here in the USA. As our smallish group was sitting around, a couple asked if I was the one that the town turned against years ago. Really? How long will this story live in infamy of island lore? Now, not really sure if they were friend or foe, I responded in the affirmative and gave them a sweet (hopefully it didn't look like a grimace) smile. They went on to question me about my work and how I classify myself, and it went on and on and on . . . and on.

I never felt confronted (thanks, Uriel), but never really felt that they understood and were on my side. I took a deep breath, adjusted my body so it was fully facing them, and spoke. Body language is very important as it shows/ shares exposure to our vital organs, which can be an easy kill. If you've ever had a pet, they share their level of comfort with you by exposing their under-belly. (We do the same, although it doesn't tend to be as obvious since we're not usually laying on our backs with our bellies in the air!)

I shared why I do what I do. Our conversation lasted a solid twenty minutes, and honestly, I'm still not sure they got me or approved. But then again, I'm not here to win everyone's approval. Just like you're not. During that time, I felt my blood pressure stabilize, and felt Uriel's hand on my shoulder, softly infusing me with his light.

As the conversation came to a close, it was approaching firework time. The owner of the store, a long-time believer in my gifts, asked me to give him another energy treatment while everyone was there. Such support and confirmation that it is, indeed, safe for me to be me!

Thanks again, Uriel.

Uriel's Light Temple

Uriel's light temple is located within the Tatra Mountains in southern Poland. These mountains create a natural boundary between Poland and what is now known as Slovakia. Within this majestic spot lies the resort town of Zakopane. Poles flock here to rest, ski, and commune in the beauty of this breathtaking area beckoning over 250,000 tourists annually. I was blessed to visit Zakopane years ago with my Polish grandmother. Of course, this was long before I was consciously connected to the angels and Uriel. Can you imagine my joy when I discovered Uriel's light temple is located here? I had even more of a reason to be thankful for that trip! We were in the area for three days, and during that time, events took place that made me more thankful for life as I obtained a deeper understanding of why I'm here on Earth at the present time. I had moments of feeling completely safe, to soar and just be. I now understand that these feelings were not only due to a trip of a lifetime with Grandma, but to Uriel's intercession, even if it was unbeknownst to me at that time.

Uriel's Symbol

Uriel's symbol starts deep and low. It ascends slowly. It bounces out, plateaus, even slips backward, ultimately reaching new heights and finishing in the same vertical plane, completely on track.  Think of it as a symbol for life. At times, you may get completely sidetracked from life; you get busy *doing* versus *being*; you may slip back to old ways of being; you may reach a plateau, neither slipping backward or gaining momentum forward. I actually prefer to think of this phase more as a marinade phase. It's never a bad phase, but rather a beautiful moment to allow energies, lessons, and adventures to integrate more fully. If you feel yourself slipping backward, it simply means you have not fully grasped the learning adventure or have forgotten a part of yourself that requires more embracing and lovin'. Take the time now not to rush, but to see the larger picture of the whos, whys, hows, etc. As this newfound knowledge is integrated and becomes part of who you are, you will have the energy and knowledge to catapult to the next level. Have you ever dieted and found yourself slipping off the eating regime? What about dating? Ever felt like it was the same person in a different skin? Smoking? Drugs? Negative thinking (this includes gossiping), etc.? Any area of life can be graphed using Uriel's symbol.

Uriel's Compass Direction

Uriel's compass direction is true north. North is associated with knowledge and philosophy. If you wrap these two up together, they obviously work in the region of the mind. New information and the expansion of consciousness can also be associated with religion and spirituality. Let those north winds blow! Uriel, with the help of his twin, Auriel, helps you find your true north and what drives and compels you, while helping you feel safe and secure in the knowledge of what you are here to do.

Uriel's Chakra Association

Uriel oversees the root chakra, the place of divine safety. Its location is at the base of the spine. The root chakra resonates a deep ruby red, which ironically is one of the crystals that not only supports the chakra, but supports Uriel. Your root chakra instills safety, allowing you to explore the world in all its glory.

The root chakra is also uncanny in its ability to allow you to feel a balanced expression of self, while being connected to the angelic realm. In other words, owning your sense of true self while feeling safe, secure, and grounded in its power. This contributes greatly to you sharing your amazing gifts with the universe at large, whether it's being an accountant, angel Goddess, trash collector, artist, CEO/CFO/COO (or any one of those Os). What matters is you being you, because nobody else can! This is all part of Uriel's area of expertise.

This chakra can certainly be connected with the fight-or-flight response. If you are not familiar with this response, it happens when you are placed in an unpleasant situation and must internally decide whether you wish to stand tall and fight (in the literal and/or figurative sense) or take flight. The root chakra not only encompasses safety and security, but also your physical health. Without your health, you have nothing. Think about it, if you are ill, are you living life joyously? Do you enjoy eating yummy food? How about physical activities? What about aromas? Do they now make you nauseous? And so on, and so on, and, well, you get the idea.

As an example, smell can easily trigger the fight-or-flight response; when you smell something rancid or non enticing, does it send your senses reeling, resulting in the refrigerator door slamming shut? Or running with the food-in-question outstretched, putting it as far away as possible to get it out of your arena? If some scent is detected that repels us, how long do we stick around to investigate? Typically, not long; the only desire is to be away from it.

Equally, a smell can be something to revel and bask in. It makes us stop and linger awhile. I recall a trip we took to Palm Desert, California. As the car approached the hotel, the scent of jasmine wafted across the courtyard and through the car windows. Before the car came to a full stop, I jumped out of the car to find the source. What a surprise to see that each balcony was cascading with blooming jasmine! I was in heaven.

I'm sure you can think of similar scents that make you stop in your tracks and drink in their aroma. What happens when you smell fresh-baked pie, bread, or chocolate chip cookies? What about a quart of fresh strawberries while they are in season? The smell of fresh cut grass or the ocean? These scents are soothing, enticing, and harken feelings of security, joy, and love. Lower blood pressure can easily aid in the relaxation of our entire being.

When your root chakra is balanced, you realize that you are safe to express your physical beauty and honor that temple called your body. You eat healthy, you exercise, you rest according to your needs, and not necessarily what society dictates. In other words, you feel secure with the world around you. When the root chakra is out of alignment, inner stillness becomes elusive, insecurity preys on your mind, obesity can be an ongoing issue, as well as greediness. Yuck! Not a way I wish to live my life! Don't you agree? I choose security, inner knowing, and restful existence. Are you with me?

As the root chakra is located at the base of the spine, it is also the fundamental chakra within the kundalini yoga philosophy called the breath of fire (yet another nod to Uriel's name). Through this specialized breathing technique, you can raise your personal fire energy up your spine to become more empowered and enlightened with the universe around you.

Angel Activity

Uriel's activity is one you can do daily from this moment forward. He actually suggests two.

1. Begin using the daily Askfirmation, *Why is it safe for me to be me?* This one Askfirmation is a game changer for the rest of your life. I and many clients have literally gotten taller. Why? It's certainly not because I'm exercising better (I did study ballet for eleven years and still do yoga); it's because I feel more confident and more empowered with my mission than ever. Countless folks have told me they love watching me walk. Even more have mentioned that I've gotten taller! I finally confirmed it at the doctor: I have indeed grown one inch!

2. Do something, even if it seems inconsequential, that is new for you each day. Sometimes it's simply changing your walking/jogging route. Sometimes, it's speaking your mind (in the most loving way possible, of course). Sometimes, it's really going out there and going after your dreams with complete abandon. Bottom line, Uriel is with you to remind you that you can do this today and every day from now on. He's got your back to remind you that you are safe to be you and to share all aspects of yourself with the world at large.

Uriel's Healing Crystals

As mentioned, the ruby is one of Uriel's go-to crystals. Don't worry, there are many rough rubies out there, so no need to purchase a high-quality gem, but if you desire to do so, go ahead! A ruby connects with spiritual wisdom; it is akin to royalty. It brings an enthusiasm for life to the forefront. It symbolizes the sun, and its glowing hue suggests an inextinguishable flame that legends claim would shine through even the thickest clothing and could not be hidden. What a beautiful metaphor for you; shine your essence! Ruby is known to promote a clear mind, increased concentration and motivation, and a sense of confidence and determination that can overcome timidity.

Another crystal that works with Uriel's energy is the magenta garnet. Many use this stone for psychic protection as well as physical love. Garnet is easily found in all forms of jewelry, and this is quite beneficial as it is also known to help advance your chosen career. You know those feelings of helplessness that can creep in during the middle of night? Garnet is your go-to crystal for easing those thoughts and eliminating any kind of self-sabotage by helping you feel safer to be you in all arenas of your life.

Uriel's Aromatherapy

Some of Uriel's scents are:

Red Mandarin (there's that red, again!): known to help calm not only rambunctious children but to alleviate acne and sharpen the mind.
Frankincense: has energy that assists to ground you while expanding the soul.

Oil of Pettigraine: offers antiseptic qualities to help keep your space pure, as in, no longer having baggage to carry with you; once again allowing you to stand tall and feel safe to be you.

Uriel's Askfirmations

Why is it safe for me to be me?

Why is it so easy to embrace my blessing?

Why is it so easy to fly my freak flag?

Uriel Fun Facts

★ He told Noah of the impending flood and how to prepare.

★ Uriel is often associated with lightning storms. Talk about drastic and sudden action!

★ Uriel's musical note is a C, as in "Cowabonga, it's really cool to be here!"

Guided Meditation with Archangel Uriel

Sit facing north.

Breathe in,
Hold for four counts,
Breathe out.

Set your intention to strengthen your connection with Archangel Uriel.

Breathe in,
Hold for four counts,
Breathe out.

Your eyes soften,
Your breath deepens,
Your body relaxes.

Breathe in,
Hold for four counts,
Breathe out.

A light begins to glow,
It warms your body,
As it fills the room.

Breathe in,
Hold for four counts,
Breathe out.

You see a hand holding the flame.
The palm presents itself as you are most comfortable,
Upright with the flame resting,
Facing you with the flame embedded in the palm.

Breathe in,
Hold for four counts,
Breathe out.

You notice within the flame a person.
This person looks familiar.
You realize it is you!

Breathe in,
Hold for four counts,
Breathe out.

You feel the warmth of the flame surrounding you.

Breathe in.
Hold for four counts.
Breathe out.

As the flame helps to burn off old beliefs,
You are like the phoenix bird rising from the ashes.

Breathe in,
Hold for four counts,
Breathe out.

You are shining,
You are glowing,
You are safe to be you.

Breathe in,
Hold for four counts,
Breathe out.

The fire's energy continues to swirl and slough off what is no longer needed,
By you.

Breathe in,
Hold for four counts,
Breathe out.

As each mindset turns to ash,
You feel reborn,
Renewed,
Safe.

Breathe in,
Hold for four counts,
Breathe out.

You stand tall,
Arms by your side,
Palms facing front.

Breathe in,
Hold for four counts,
Breathe out.

You smile with that inner knowing of who you are,
And what you are here to do.

Breathe in,
Hold for four counts,
Breathe out.

Repeat.

Breathe in,
Hold for four counts,
Breathe out.

You are ready to step out of today's meditation.

Breathe in,
Hold for four counts,
Breathe out.

The light before you and surrounding you begins to dim.

Breathe in,
Hold for four counts,
Breathe out.

You are smiling that Mona Lisa smile.

Breathe in,
Hold for four counts,
Breathe out.

The noises in your environment become louder.
You feel your physical body within the room.

Breathe in,
Hold for four counts,
Breathe out.

Your eyes softly open and close.
You stretch your hands and feet.

Breathe in,
Hold for four counts,
Breathe out.

You stretch your body,
And fully open your eyes.

Welcome back!

4

Archangel Gabriel (Gabe or Gabi)

Angel of Miracles

"Grace Always Begins Inside."

—Archangel Gabriel

Toot, Toot! That is Gabriel tooting his horn with you in mind. Gabriel is often portrayed carrying a horn, as he is known as the great communicator. He brings news of all kinds: the good, the bad, the ugly, and the euphoric. He is the angel responsible for giving Mary the news of the impending birth of her Son. Talk about euphoric, but what a burden knowing what your son was to experience in his life. Gabriel's horn can also offer the all's-good-to-go sign. In fact, while at an expo, a new client came forward only because she heard Gabriel's horn while standing at our booth and knew she would get great clarity from the angels through me. What a blessing!

Gabriel also assists in awakening the senses. For example, think of one of the most decadent meals you've ever had. You felt the food swirl around the inside of your mouth; the textures, the spices. The food felt like it was literally exploding and made you salivate for more. This is the senses waking up and truly enjoying what life is offering you. The meal became a sensual experience, just like wearing a luxurious piece of clothing or smelling an aroma you adore.

Want to be more creative? Gabriel is your angel. You can and are creative in the day-to-day of life too! Don't believe me? What about problem solving, cleaning, orchestrating multiple schedules, and more? How many times have you come up with a solution to get something done more efficiently? That's Gabriel at work.

How about those doodles you absentmindedly draw when bored? What about how you decorate your home? So, the next time someone says you or they are not creative, just smile and shout out, "Au contraire," and give a wink to Gabriel for showing you how creative you really are.

Gabriel assists in birth as well as death. It's the cycle/circle of Life. He is especially helpful if the grieving process has become difficult and you can't get past the death of a loved one or beloved pet. Whether it is mourning, blaming yourself for things said or not said, things done or not done, all those "what ifs" that typically run amuck during this powerfully charged time, allow Gabriel to connect with you and remember the joyful moments of that one's life and the reason they were in it, no matter how short or long. If there is something that is still yearning to be said to them, Gabriel can and will assist getting your message delivered. Remember that he carries a horn—it acts as a great megaphone.

Gabriel is the ruler of the cherubim and virtues, bestowing grace to those who need courage and inspiration. As you embark upon any creative endeavor, call on Gabriel and harness the energies of the sun, the moon, and stars with the assistance of the cherubim. While creating, connecting to the virtues suspends the law of nature to create miracles on Earth. What a beautiful platform for those creative endeavors and getting them out into the world!

For those involved in television, radio, or any form of communication for that matter, be sure to chat with Gabriel. It is through creative expression that we typically are the most powerful, for those interactions are the most memorable. Think about when you were back in school. Which teachers connected more deeply to you? The ones who droned on or the ones who were interactive and creative in their presentation? Same goes for the movies. The most profound actors can share the deepest message through humor.

Zodiac Association

Gabriel connects with the zodiac sign of Cancer, the crab. Crabs may have a shell of protection surrounding them, but they feel all that comes toward them. They are alive; their sense of feeling is quite profound and at times it is unfortunately necessary to retreat in order to regroup. Connecting with the energy of Cancer along with Gabriel's energy helps one feel alive in all arenas of their life.

Gabriel's Name Defined

Gabriel's name translates to "God is my strength." What a beautiful reminder that you can build your strength with the assistance of Gabriel. Strength to go after your dreams. Strength to give birth to new ways of being. Strength to be different, to be you. Strength to not only shine, but to share your brilliance with the world.

Gabriel's Light Temple

I'm purposely switching up the order for Gabriel's section as my angelic encounter happened while at his light temple. Gabriel's light temple is located at Mt. Shasta, California. It is a beautiful area, pristine in energy, almost over-powering with the love it exudes. The town of Mt. Shasta has crystal shops and UFOs galore. Yes, you read correctly, many of Shasta's respectable citizens have witnessed UFOs coming in and out of the mountain via spaceships or some sort of energy vehicle. Some say it is Lemurians that have survived, some say extraterrestrials, some freely say they have no clue what or who it is. Until you experience it yourself, it remains speculation and open for you to decide who and or what is visiting us.

Angelic Encounter

I was blessed to visit Mt. Shasta years ago with two newfound friends. I had just met them at a conference and we blew (excuse the pun, Gabriel) off the last day just so we could head south and experience Mt. Shasta and its loving energies. Off we went on this grand adventure. We traversed the town, visited crystal stores, and had a lovely lunch. All the while we could see the beauty of the mountain from every angle. The yearnings started and we just had to go on the mountain herself. However, time was an issue. The other two women had a flight to catch back to their home turf, but Mt. Shasta called. We listened, and trusted that we could visit and get back in time for them to catch their flight home.

Up the mountain we drove. We found the perfect spot to pull over and hopped out of the car to breathe in the beauty. The driver said we had ten minutes *max* to stop, and that was still cutting it close. The view was breathtaking. The air was crisp. The flowers danced. The wind caressed our bodies. We felt the love exuding not only from the mountain, but I now know from Gabriel, as well. Our senses became alive. While the energy was certainly charged, we all felt very present and balanced. The three of us separated to say our prayers of thanks privately.

The driver pulled back and got in the car. Trying to be conscientious, I finished up my prayers and got in the car as well, not wanting to delay them, but the third person seemed to not have a care in the world. She stayed outside. I started fidgeting. I was getting nervous for them. How inconsiderate of this woman to take so long! She continued to do whatever ritual she was called to do. Surely, we had gone far past ten minutes! We had to be bordering on fifteen to twenty minutes or maybe twenty-five minutes, at least. My fingers started tapping my knees, I started nibbling on my lower lip in anticipation. They would miss their flight! Very serenely, she eventually got back in the car. The driver started the car, and lo and behold, when I saw the car clock, we had been out ten minutes, *exactly*. Who says they can't stop time when necessary?

Thank you, Gabriel.

Gabriel's Symbol

Look at his symbol. Unlike Uriel's symbol that starts low to take you higher, Gabriel's starts high and digs deep only to rise again. The acknowledgement and loving of what you are hiding, especially toward yourself, can have you soaring in no time. Going deep into the psyche can be a daunting experience, *only* if you think it so. Remember, going deeper only unveils the true essence of you and therefore

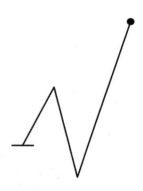

unleashes the creative juices that can and will affect all arenas of your life. Each rise is empowering, allowing you to dig a bit deeper on the next trip down, leaving you to shine more brilliantly than ever before. Each dip strengthens you. Each discovery is empowering and gives you courage to toot your horn with greater knowing.

How to dig deep with grace? Allow yourself to be there. It is a different kind of ride to visit and see what has been hidden for days, weeks, or perhaps years within you. However, by opening the door to allow more aspects of you to venture forth only makes the world a more joyous place—because it starts with you. Ask a few questions that you wish clarity in. Write down the questions and release the answering portion to Gabriel. Don't judge or second-guess the answers as they come in; simply jot them down. Remember, you were stumped. Obviously, what you are already aware of isn't the answer, so being creative in obtaining the results you desire is just the ticket!

Gabriel's Compass Direction

Gabriel's compass direction is the west, typically associated with death. If that's the case, and it is, how can he also symbolize birth? One way to think about it is that with every death, there is a birth or a rebirth. Remember, death isn't always physical. It can be the end of a way of life; changing eating habits, thought patterns, etc. West is also known to be the gateway of emotions, inspiration (think of how a sunset can make you stop in awe and wonder), and, of course, change. Think of the brave people who headed west time and time again in an effort to enhance their life. Crystals you can add to Gabriel's altar are citrine and orange calcite. Citrine helps bring in the richness of life on all levels to help you feel more alive and embrace the sparkles, nuances, and joys. Through orange calcite's gentleness, you can begin to own your sensuality as well as your many creative talents.

Gabriel's Chakra Association

Gabriel oversees the sacral chakra located in the approximate area of your navel. The sacral chakra color is akin to the ripest orange dripping with the juices of life. Oh, the angelic humor! I purchased flowers today to brighten up my office area. They were arranged beautifully in a crystal vase, and when I sat down to write, I found it was time for Gabriel's chapter. As I started writing, my eyes fell on the vase of flowers. What color? Orange, of course. One must love the angels' sense of humor and never-ending ways they wish to connect with us.

The sacral chakra oversees the birthing aspect on all levels and offers clues to our reproductive organs and how we view them. Humans give physical birth. Authors give birth to their books. Every artist gives birth to their creation. Even if you don't consider yourself an artist, you still give birth; perhaps you moved to start a new life. Perhaps you started a new eating regime to start anew and get healthier. In other words, it is a way of introducing a new concept, new way of being, a new way to express one's self.

When a sacral chakra is more balanced, you'll love feeling the texture of quality clothing next to your body, caressing the softness of pure cotton, silk, or linen. The man-made materials simply don't feel as good as they once did. Your creative juices will flow in all areas of your life, from practical problem-solving to the truly artistic. When the sacral is out of balance, you will feel frustration quicker and creativity will be blocked. Feelings of isolation may prevail as well as sexual frigidness or the opposite: sexual promiscuity and/or lower back issues. Allow the water energies of your sacral chakra to encase you, just like when you were in the womb, to lovingly rock you and bring a sense of security to these areas of your life.

Angelic Activity

As you are picking up on Gabriel's energy and mission, he invites you to become more alive! There are so many ways to do this:

★ Honor your body as you bathe; use great products that make you feel, well, great! Soothing lotions, creams, etc. Feel your body thank you as you begin to honor it more.

★ Really enjoy your meals. How often, in this fast-paced world, is food simply inhaled, leaving a small pile of rocks in the pit of your stomach? No more. On the road? Surely you can spare twenty minutes of time to find a healthier place to nourish your body and soul. We are on the road a lot and can often find some independent place that has great food.

★ Look at your clothes. Do they reflect your truest essence or are they a cry for help and attention? Yes, this harkens a bit to Michael's assignment of clutter clearing, but as you continue to evolve, love what you put on your body, too!

So, for Gabriel, there isn't just one assignment, but rather a bevy of ways to be more sensual. When your senses come alive, you begin to allow those creative juices to flow more easily to all arenas of your life, from the mundane (looking for creative solutions) to the artistic.

Gabriel's Healing Crystals

Gabriel resonates with the beautiful, glowing crystal orange calcite. Orange calcite brings playfulness with it while opening gateways for creativity, dismissing shame when connected to sexuality, and embracing regeneration, confidence, and innovation. Orange calcite's vital energy can serve as a catalyst for the release of past traumas that have been holding you back, allowing for optimism and joy to come in. Depressed? This crystal can help wake up your senses with a sense of vitality. The calcite family is very soft in their power. Remember, never underestimate the power of softness, for therein lies the truest strength!

Another crystal choice for Gabriel is citrine. Most citrine is a lab-heated amethyst, but as it is heated, its molecular structure shifts and resonates from that moment on as citrine. Citrine is a beautiful, sparkly stone that is a deep amber color. Isn't it funny that the word sparkly was used? That's you at the core—a very, very sparkly human that is meant and designed to shine their brilliance with the world! Citrine is well known as a happy stone, gently making its surroundings purer, therefore happier. Citrine is also associated with alleviating self-destructive tendencies that can prevent you from achieving all that is truly desired.

Angelic Aromatherapy

Some of Gabriel's favorite scents are:

Myrrh: one of the holiest of plants and assists in purification and letting go of the past.

Ylang Ylang: brings in optimism while lifting sadness and opening to the possibility of the angelic realms and feeling worthy to receive it.

Neroli: acts as an antidepressant, helping you feel more alive.

Sweet Orange: also acts as an antidepressant, but as an aphrodisiac to boot!

Gabriel's Askfirmations

Why is it so easy for me to embrace my creativity?

Why is it so easy for me to find a creative solution to _____?

Why is it so easy for me to embrace my sensual side?

Gabriel's Fun Facts

★ Wolves are known symbols of Gabriel. Think of those pioneers heading west again. What would they frequently hear at night serenading them? Wolves. Wolves, while perhaps sounding desolate, were actually serenading them as they birthed their new life.

★ Gabriel is associated with the musical note of D, as in "Dang, I'm Ahmazing" (or whatever other expletive you choose to throw in).

★ Believe it or not, Gabriel is also associated with certain trees. Some of the more well-known ones are the weeping willow. Oh, how I loved climbing in one as a child! Another is the pear tree; this would also then apply to fruit. Perhaps drinking pear juice or munching on a pear while in a creative mode can open your channel to Gabriel in the birthing of your project!

Guided Meditation with Archangel Gabriel

Sit facing west.

Breathe in,
Hold for four counts,
Breathe out.

Call on Archangel Michael and his legions,
To stand guard while you meditate.

Breathe in,
Hold for four counts,
Breathe out.

The room fills.
It gets warmer,
As Michael and his legion enter to stand guard,
During this meditation.

Breathe in,
Hold for four counts,
Breathe out.

It is now time to call on,
Archangel Gabriel.

Breathe in,
Hold for four counts,
Breathe out.

Feel a stirring in your sacral chakra,
As Gabriel enters your sacred space.

Breathe in,
Hold for four counts,
Breathe out.

As you continue to breathe,
Gabriel officially enters the room.

Breathe in,
Hold for four counts,
Breathe out.

The space surrounding you feels more alive,
And yet,
Grounded.

Breathe in,
Hold for four counts,
Breathe out.

Gabriel steps closer.
You feel a warmth emanating from him.

Breathe in,
Hold for four counts,
Breathe out.

Even with your eyes softly closed,
You see the brightness.

Breathe in,
Hold for four counts,
Breathe out.

Gabriel asks,
"How may I help you?"

Breathe in,
Hold for four counts,
Breathe out.

You share one area of your life,
For which you would like a creative solution.

Breathe in,
Hold for four counts,
Breathe out.

Gabriel steps closer,
And gently takes your hands in one of his.

Breathe in,
Hold for four counts,
Breathe out.

With his other hand,
He gently lifts your face and asks that you open your eyes.

Breathe in,
Hold for four counts,
Breathe out.

As you open your eyes,
You see before you the eyes of Gabriel.

Breathe in,
Hold for four counts,
Breathe out.

He now shares with you,
Many possible solutions to your situation.

Breathe in,
Hold for four counts,
Breathe out.

As he shares, each one is infused within your being,
So you will remember them all.

Breathe in,
Hold for four counts,
Breathe out.

He gently raises one hand,
To softly close your eyes once more.

Breathe in,
Hold for four counts,
Breathe out.

Both of your hands are now placed back on your lap.

Breathe in,
Hold for four counts,
Breathe out.

He whispers,
"You are Loved,"
In your ear.

Breathe in,
Hold for four counts,
Breathe out.

As his energy begins to dissipate,
You are reminded that you may call upon him,
At any time.

Breathe in,
Hold for four counts,
Breathe out.

Gabriel steps further away,
And your sacral chakra is fully energized and balanced.

Breathe in,
Hold for four counts,
Breathe out.

Gabriel continues his retreat,
And as he does so, the noises in the room become louder.

Breathe in,
Hold for four counts,
Breathe out.

You take a deep inhale and exhale loudly.

Breathe in,
Hold for four counts,
Breathe out.

You gently open your eyes,
And wiggle your fingers and toes.

Breathe in,
Hold for four counts,
Breathe out.

You are back in the present,
Fully alert,
And grounded.

Breathe in,
Hold for four counts,
Breathe out.

5

Archangel Jophiel (Josie)

Angel of Joy-Filled Power

"Be happy, Be silly! Be you!"

—Archangel Jophiel

Jophiel helps you find your bliss. Bliss? Perfect happiness; a state of spiritual connection that wraps you in such a sense of purity and love that many are brought to a teary-eyed state of being. Whenever you are feeling totally Zen and experiencing *one*, that's Jophiel.

When you desire something, I mean really desire to the point where you can envision, taste, feel, and know it, but are not stepping into it, Jophiel is your go-to angel. She (I "see" Jophiel as a "she") can be quite creative in getting you not only motivated once again, but to find the joy to keep you focused. This book is a perfect example. I'd been working on it but got sidetracked with clients, product development, opportunities, etc., and it sat for a few years as the energies marinated and I grew more comfortable about being the authority to share this knowledge with you.

Enter Jophiel to this scenario. Within the span of a few weeks, several clients and would-be clients inquired about a 101 book and how to better understand and connect with the angelic realm. They expressed a strong desire to study under me, and, well, the rest is history. I got the book going once more and it became a win-win.

Jophiel also assists as the intellectual stimulant. Want to learn new things, but feeling sluggish? Chat with Jophiel. Want some help with concentrating? Chat with Jophiel. Learning anything new, you got it; chat with Jophiel. She really is better than coffee.

As with all of the angels, Jophiel assists in various emotional human attributes. Some of the more well-known ones include laughter, joy, and being able to see the beauty in all. Seeing the trend yet? Are you better able to understand a bit more why she's been dubbed the joy-filled angel? Through this joy, you see and can embrace the beauty in all circumstances. You can see and embrace the higher learning adventure that is being offered. You can see and embrace the blessing of each event and not get caught up in the human aspect of the bad and ugly, or in other words, the ego.

As an example, the next time you see a negative post on social media or the news, instead of feeling the not-so-great energies being exuded, step back so you can better understand those higher messages. You can better understand the whys and why nots with greater joy. Through that joy, you are better able to help more, especially yourself.

Flip this mindset around and think of a time when you were hanging out with your friends and/or family and just laughing and having a good time. How did you feel? You most likely felt like you. There was no agenda. There was no second-guessing. You were beautiful you. Empowered. Therefore, some of Jophiel's other gifts include raising self-esteem. When you are feeling more empowered, your self-esteem naturally rises. She also assists in self-control. This area covers many areas, such as food: eating to nourish, not out of boredom, anxiety, compulsion, etc. Self-control can certainly include self-indulgence in any facet of life: shopping, drugs, sex, even self-pity! Self-control can also include temper, staying within the expansiveness of your heart, not shifting into the confines and bitterness of the ego. Jophiel will remind you that these are all temporary fixes for the root of what's going on in your life. She reminds you to stay centered and focused on the energy of joy that comes from within.

Archangel Jophiel assists in not only helping you to step more fully and confidently into your power, she also assists greatly in strengthening your connection to your higher self (think your soul), all of your guides, and, what a surprise . . . the angels.

Zodiac Association

The zodiac sign of Libra connects with Jophiel. Librans are known to appreciate the beauty of all; a true nod to Jophiel, whose name means "beauty of God." Librans tend to be very balanced, or at least have a better handle on the imbalance of things and strive to bring the beauty back tenfold. Librans tend to be *on* at all times; assisting, sharing, and helping others. Jophiel reminds Librans to keep things in balance; it's okay to honor your beauty, too! What are your needs and desires? It's okay to ask and receive assistance.

Jophiel's Name Defined

Archangel Jophiel's name means "beauty of God." What a perfect name for this glorious angel as she helps you release and radiate your inner beauty to continue your personal empowerment dance simply by incorporating more joy into your life. How can it get any better than that?

Angelic Encounter

My encounter with Jophiel didn't happen to me directly, as you will read, but was rather relayed via our dentist to my husband. I'm naturally a happy person and can see the beauty in the simplest and most intricate of things. It's a rare photo or time when you don't see me smiling. After we moved to a new city, we naturally acquired a new dentist. At my first dental consultation, the new dentist treated me from start to finish to allow him to get to know me as a person, not just a patient. We simply hit it off. We chatted the entire time and it felt like kindred spirits had reunited. He shared his personal history with me, and the consultation ended with us practically hugging each other. He's a great guy and very inspiring.

A few months later, my honey went in for his first visit to the same dental practice. The dentist treated him from start to finish. Upon meeting, our dentist promptly asked, "Is your wife always so happy?"

"Yes, and there are no drugs involved!"

Joy, anyone? Chat with Jophiel to keep this energy close at all times.

Jophiel's Light Temple

Jophiel's light temple is in Lanchow, China. While never having been to China, I do thoroughly enjoy good Chinese food. Do you think that counts? Yes, a bit of poor Chatter humor going on.

Jophiel's Symbol

Look at Jophiel's symbol. It starts far left, heads up and right, shoots up at an angle, and then finishes straight down. Think of yourself as the north/south line. You are the strong beam of light that the symbol encases. Jophiel's symbol starts behind you (the back door), grabbing your power and joy that you have kept hidden. The power and joy stream through you (at the solar plexus area) and push outward to be shared with the world. It then shoots over your crown, more to the soul star chakra location, and grabs the universal energy to bring down and permeate all the cells within your body. As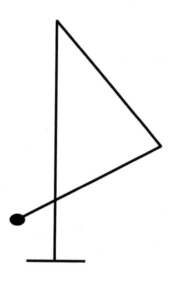
it cascades downward, it grows and shines beyond your feet. This allows your joy, your power, to anchor firmly into the earth. Through this anchoring, you will walk confidently in joy. One way to think of it is empowered joy, or put in another way, joyfully empowered.

Jophiel's Compass Direction

Jophiel's compass direction is northwest. This direction is also associated with learning new and retaining old information, and putting it into action. Therefore, if you or someone you know is a student, suggest that they face northwest while studying. While not always possible, you can use one of Jophiel's crystals and place it/them in that area while studying (it will help with retention) and then carry with you during exam time.

　　Don't fret, we'll get into Jophiel's crystal of choice in just a few moments; stay with me.

Jophiel's Chakra Association

Based on the above, are you surprised that Jophiel's chakra is the solar plexus? While Michael also oversees this chakra, they address it from different energies that beautifully overlap and support the other. Working in tandem, Michael acts as the quintessential big brother: protector, guardian, advisor, and practical joker (just wait, his sense of humor is legendary). Jophiel on the other wing is full of empowering joy. This is the very reason she is called the joy-filled angel. Jophiel gets you into your power through the back door, through joy.

If you had to describe joy in a color, it most likely would coincide with the solar plexus chakra color. This chakra is dazzling yellow and located in your abdominal region, slightly above your naval. It offers glimpses of wisdom on how you view yourself and how you are able to wield your personal power. Think back to a time when you felt out of your element or threatened. You most likely crossed your arms over your body. This is a natural instinct that humans do to protect themselves energetically; most don't even realize they are doing it. However, when this posture is held, the message is sent out: *You cannot have my power! I am not giving it away!* How smart you are to do this intuitively.

This also supports how Jophiel presents herself. Jophiel is often seen holding a brilliant yellow orb that aligns with the placement of the solar plexus chakra. This orb pulsates, radiates, and glows outwardly for the world to see. What a beautiful symbol and reminder that your power is your center. Hold it gently and support it and the universe and all of its occupants will take note.

Your solar plexus chakra illuminates mental power, vitality, confidence, as well as intellectual activity, joy, laughter, and anger. There are many phrases that are commonly used in connection with this chakra, such as, "I'm sick to my stomach." You felt like all power had left you to the point you may have literally gotten ill with nausea. Another popular phrase is, "my gut instinct."

Then there are those coveted days when all is possible and you know you can do anything you put your mind and heart to. It all depends on how balanced the chakra is at that moment in time. Remember, you are your most powerful when you are in your joy. Simply meaning that when in joy, you are not domineering or bossy. Being empowered *is* joyful. Empowerment brings you a life that is full of laughter and true possibilities. Living with eyes wide open helps you go after your dreams and see them come to fruition. That renewed vigor? Joy. Are you beginning to see and understand why joy is such an important ingredient in not only chatting with the angels, but living life on your own terms?

When the solar plexus chakra is in balance, you feel confident, energized, strong, you can conquer anything in your path or put your mind to! When it is out of alignment, you can become domineering, aggressive, or overly sensitive, and display self-deprecating tendencies. Physical ailments can include diabetes, chronic fatigue, and ulcers. Such a powerful chakra (excuse the pun).

Angelic Activity: The Joy Challenge

Jophiel's activity is a challenge activity. Remember, she reminds you that you are your most powerful in your joy; therefore, the joy challenge is to reconnect with that inner joy. I know, I know, so much easier said than done at times, but stay with me. As you have by now figured out, we can be and are very busy. We pride ourselves often on how much we accomplish in any given day. Jophiel, along with the rest of the gang members, is here to remind you to stop and smell those lovely roses and reconnect with you through the essence of love and joy.

For the next week: no more multi-tasking. This is a bit harder than you may think. Especially with the use of cell phones, Bluetooth devices, etc. How easy is it to drive and chat away? I know I'm guilty of that. When you drive, you drive. When you eat, you eat; no driving and eating, no watching TV and eating. When you chat on the phone, sit and be present. It's in the nuances of conversations that great joy is present. Giggle, have fun, and share with your friends and family.

The second and last part of your challenge is to find one thing to laugh at daily. This does not mean to laugh at someone's expense; not good juju. Rather, to laugh when you find the humor in any given situation. As an example, I make myself a daily cappuccino using an AeroPress machine that includes a metal strainer. The angels and faeries thought to play a joke on me today; they hid the strainer. I turned the kitchen upside down and even went outside looking for it (I dump the coffee grounds daily on the gardens). Zip, zero, nada. On day three, the strainer magically appeared in the dish rack. Now, I checked it at least six times and it wasn't there. I'm the only human in the house at the moment, so no human was playing jokes on me. I could have flipped out over the missing strainer, but came up with creative ideas (thanks, Gabriel) to make the coffee. Once found, we all had a good laugh with ample eye rolling.

Moral of the story? When you are in a moment of joy, there is nothing wrong. You are present. You are you, a very empowered and loving soul.

Jophiel's Healing Crystals

If being empowered still brings in those butterflies of squeamishness and uncertainties, yellow calcite is a great crystal choice and resonates beautifully with Jophiel. The entire calcite family is a soft energetic crystal. Not as soft as a down pillow, but it literally feels like a silk skin. There is a calcite for every chakra color/mission and this makes it the perfect crystal for beginners and those who have true internal fear of empowerment on any level. The gentleness of the calcite family is sublime, but oh the power within that softness!

Yellow calcite does just that, reminds you that you can be soft in your power. Being soft or gentle does not equate with you being a wimp. You can be joyful in your power. Giving yourself permission to be empowered is just the beginning of a glorious, fun, swanky, and sexy ride. The strong, gentle energies that yellow calcite offers makes it a perfect match for those dealing with empowerment issues, as it slowly and lovingly takes you on a ride of divine self-discovery and gently coaxes you into the empowerment ride of a lifetime.

Angelic Aromatherapy

Speaking of uplifting spirits, try incorporating **Bergamot** into your routine if you are looking for a boost in your self-confidence. **Sweet orange** is a lovely scent to connect with Jophiel and her mission of joy. Orange heralds in a newness, cleansing the area and bringing with it a sense of purpose with undertones of joy. If you have undergone a severe past trauma, which I certainly hope you have not, use some juniper. **Juniper** has been known to dispel negative energy and eradicates past trauma while allowing you to feel more protected and secure so you can walk confidently. How to do this? There are a variety of ways: candles, live bushes in your yard, and/or oil added to your bath or body oil. Remember this: never underestimate the power of a happy person!

Jophiel's Askfirmations

Why is it so easy for me to stand joyfully in my power?
Why am I embracing joy daily?
Why am I a gift to the universe?

Jophiel's Fun Facts

★ Falcon is Jophiel's animal symbol. The falcon symbolizes liberty, freedom, and victory. You are free and victorious when you are joyfully in your power.

★ Jophiel dances to the musical note E as you are so *Empowered*, with joy, of course.

Guided Meditation with Archangel Jophiel

Sit facing northwest.

Breathe in,
Hold for four counts,
Breathe out.

Call on Archangel Michael and his legions,
To stand guard while you meditate.

Breathe in,
Hold for four counts,
Breathe out.

The room fills.
It gets warmer as,
Michael and his legion enter to stand guard,
During this meditation.

Breathe in,
Hold for four counts,
Breathe out.

It is now time to call on,
Archangel Jophiel.

Breathe in,
Hold for four counts,
Breathe out.

As Jophiel enters,
She is preceded by a glowing yellow orb.

Breathe in,
Hold for four counts,
Breathe out.

She holds the orb in front of you,
As an offering.

Breathe in,
Hold for four counts,
Breathe out.

As you concentrate on the orb's energy,
You feel warmth starting within your solar plexus.

Breathe in,
Hold for four counts,
Breathe out.

The warmth feels comforting.
The warmth feels smooth and soothing.
The warmth feels strong.

Breathe in,
Hold for four counts,
Breathe out.

As you get comfortable with this energy,
It begins to enter your body,
Empowering it and bringing,
Great joy with it.

Breathe in,
Hold for four counts,
Breathe out.

The orb's only mission is to bring you,
More into your joy-filled power.

Breathe in,
Hold for four counts.
Breathe out.

Bringing with it the essence of,
Joy,
And the ability to rise above and see joy manifesting,
In all aspects of your life.

Breathe in,
Hold for four counts,
Breathe out.

Feel the joy permeating.
Feel the power that comes with joy.
Feel your essence coming more alive.

Breathe in,
Hold for four counts,
Breathe out.

As this joy takes hold,
Squeeze your thumb nail into your pinky nail.
This reminds you that joy is a state of being that you adore.

Breathe in,
Hold for four counts,
Breathe out.

Repeat.

Breathe in,
Hold for four counts,
Breathe out.

The joy continues to traverse to all parts of your body,
Ultimately leaving you with a large smile.

Breathe in,
Hold for four counts,
Breathe out.

You feel at peace.
You feel at one with the universe.
You feel love.

Breathe in,
Hold for four counts,
Breathe out.

You now own peace.
You own the Oneness.
You own the love.
For it is you.

Breathe in,
Hold for four counts,
Breathe out.

Jophiel steps back, but leaves the orb within.

Breathe in,
Hold for four counts,
Breathe out.

The orb is now permanently within you,
Always there to offer you,
The energy of joy-filled power.

Breathe in,
Hold for four counts,
Breathe out.

You begin to become more aware of the room around you.

Breathe in,
Hold for four counts,
Breathe out.

You take a deep inhale and exhale loudly.

Breathe in,
Hold for four counts,
Breathe out.

You gently open your eyes,
Wiggle your fingers and toes.

Breathe in,
Hold for four counts,
Breathe out.

You are back in the present,
Fully alert,
And grounded.

Breathe in,
Hold for four counts,
Breathe out.

6

Archangel Raphael (Ralphie, Ralph, the Docta')

Angel of Healing

"You are worthy of receiving healing on all levels. Allow me in to help you."

—Archangel Raphael

Just as Michael is my go-to for protection and strength, Archangel Raphael is my go-to for healing and relationships. Raphael is considered the doctor of the angelic realm and loves to assist in healing all aspects of your life. It's why I've nicknamed him the docta'.

Raphael is also well known as the relationship angel. Keep in mind that relationships can cover many spheres of life, such as the love kind (soul mates, twin flames, etc.), social, work, neighborhood, one could even make an argument for social media! You also have a relationship with health, money, and best of all, yourself. Yes, you have a relationship with yourself. How well do you really know *you*? Each of these areas can affect all areas of life and all can certainly benefit from healing.

Like Michael, Raphael is usually depicted carrying an item. In Raphael's case, he carries a cup, an urn, or a vial of healing salve. This salve can and does heal all, from the minor scrape to the terminal disease. Remember, he is the physician of the angelic realm, and therefore is very prominent in all healing places; hospitals, funeral homes, assisted-living facilities, healing centers, massage studios, schools, etc. If the business is designed around healing, Raphael is there, no questions asked. While Raphael is often shown carrying a vial, he is equally shown not carrying it. In those circumstances, his hand is often raised, as in administering a blessing(s). He blesses all who ask for it by sending out healing in the form of love so those receiving may walk their walk with greater conviction and compassion for all, especially themselves.

Raphael is one of the four archangels mentioned in the bible. His name translates to mean "God has healed." How fantastic is it to remember that God/Goddess heals all and that the power lies within you? It is up to you to feel worthy enough to heal and allow healing to take place. Remember, illness can stem from an energy imbalance from a place within. Once blossomed, the illness will not heal fully unless the patient feels worthy to heal what has birthed the illness. Why wouldn't one feel worthy? Great question, and the answer can be very deep—perhaps they feel responsible or guilty for something, but no matter how loud they ask, they will not heal. No matter how extensive the treatments, they shall not heal. They may rally, but the disease can still claim them.

Let's delve into this a bit more. Many often ask why they or a loved one does not heal when Raphael is called upon or healing is requested. This is truly a tough question to answer, but I shall do my best.

Take self, first. Whenever we get ill, from a minor cold to something like a twisted ankle or worse, there is something out of alignment within us. Take the twisted ankle as an example. Moving too fast through life and not appreciating the minor things could cause a twisted ankle. It can also indicate a deep thought process of not feeling supported—no leg to stand on, so to speak. Of course, the ankle will gently remind you of this. You become weak and are forced to hobble along (not very pleasantly), however, it offers a moment to reevaluate life, as it were, and see how to alter courses more to your liking.

A cold? The flu? How often have you heard, "It made me stop and rest"? The human body is a glorious thing. It constantly sends out clues when headed to a danger zone. Feelings of lethargy, exhaustion, lack of drive or focus, food not agreeing with our system, etc.; when these warning signs go unheeded, they get bigger and bigger and bigger until illness makes us stop and take notice.

This varies from person to person, case to case, but your body knows when something is obviously off. For example, I had a client years ago that came to me for healing purposes. She had cancer in her reproductive organs. What the angels illuminated during her first session was that she had been sexually abused as a child by a relative. A relative! This man was a trusted family member, so she had never told a soul. Up to that session, only three others knew of these incidences: her, the perpetrator, and her husband. She kept it bottled up for over thirty years. Can you see the connection from that repeated violation and the disease that manifested? It festered within and had no way to escape. Unfortunately, cancer was the final result. Once the dots were connected for her and in a short amount of time, she took her power back. She literally forgave the man.

And her cancer?

Shrinking.

Not all cancer patients have been abused, but this is just one example of how when you hold onto discord, disease can and usually will present itself. Some patients may decide to undergo this life adventure, while some may choose to assist others along their way and become a beacon of light for others to follow. The answers are as vast as the questions that surround the topic of healing. In other words, we don't know all the answers why.

What you may not know about Raphael is that he is also in charge of the guardian angels. Yes, everyone has one guardian angel, including you. This angel has been present since the beginning of time and will be there until the end of times. Many often become disconnected to this relationship and try to do everything themselves, which, of course, creates more stress. Relax into the heart's energy with the comfort of Raphael and he can help the two of you become reacquainted.

As mentioned, you have one guardian angel, but there are many more angels with you during each phase of your life. It all depends on your life's mission—why you are here, as well as what adventure you are currently experiencing. Which angels, you ask? That's what this book is illuminating for you. As you read through it, connect your own dots and you will begin to know whom to chat with for most circumstances of your glorious life.

Zodiac Association

Raphael connects with the zodiac sign of Aries. This may not initially sound right as Aries are known to be fiery and headstrong (I should know; I'm one!). However, Raphael helps one overcome those traits that may be unsavory to the public at large while helping one's soul heal and reminding them they have nothing to prove. The biggest lesson for an Aries may be learning how to be versus do. Thanks, Raphael!

Raphael's Name Defined

Are you surprised Raphael's name means "God has healed"? Didn't think you would be. Raphael is the consummate angel when connected with healing. It doesn't matter if it's healing regarding the physical, mental, emotional, or spiritual. It doesn't matter if it's for you, a loved one, an enemy, a pet, or any animal, for that matter. Healing is healing.

Angelic Encounter

This story illustrates how Raphael's symbol can get to the root of an issue, whether it is physical, mental, emotional, spiritual, or a combination of all. We had friends over to watch the ball game on TV. My friend decided the exercise ball was her seat of choice. While bouncing on the ball, she kept rubbing her shoulder. I asked if she wished for an energy treatment. She could barely contain her excitement and was thrilled to receive.

As I was treating her, I asked for the origination of this imbalance. Raphael quickly answered spiritual. I thought, *what?* She was one of the most religious people I knew, heavily involved in church activities, and simply walked her talk. So, of course, I began an internal argument with Raphael (trust me, you never win these discussions). He insisted it was spiritually based.

Okay, then.

When I was done, she asked the usual question, "What did you get?" I told her and waited for her "What, are you nuts?" response. Instead, she replied, "You couldn't be more correct! I'm having serious issues with the church right now and am in a major inner conflict at the moment."

Raphael came barreling through once more and said, "See? I told ya."

I offered an open-minded and safe, non judgmental opportunity for her to share her thoughts and feelings, which ultimately garnered her clarity on what her next steps could be. Her inner spiritual turmoil had elevated into a physical malady causing her great discomfort in the shoulder. (Left shoulder, in case you were wondering—the side of spirituality and receiving.) She felt like she had the weight of the world on her. Finally, she was able to move forward. Of course, lesson learned on my end—can't win an argument with an angel.

Raphael's Light Temple

Raphael's light temple is located in Fátima, Portugal. Many who make the pilgrimage to Fátima can feel his healing presence there, as he blankets it with his restorative powers. At this particular location, he works closely with Mother Mary to aid in the healing process of the world at large.

Raphael's Symbol

Look at Raphael's symbol; it starts low and deep within our psyche; the originating point of most illnesses. It can take no prisoners in the adventure of healing and shoots straight up and quick so it doesn't get sidetracked or embedded again. His symbol then gradually and gently slopes down to dig a bit deeper to prepare for its healing through love. Think of this as the fluffing up stage; the stage where you let go and relax enough for it/you to be healed. The

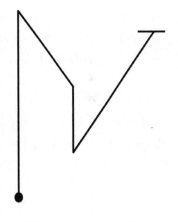

symbol then grabs on to whatever is presenting itself, whatever is no longer needed. Then, whoosh, up once more, and away. It is released from all of our bodies; the physical, mental, emotional, and spiritual.

Think of a time when you have been ill. I'm not just talking about the sniffles, here, I'm talking about the flu or some kind of illness that had you flat-out bedridden. Odds are you had a low point, a point where you knew it was the bottom; no place else to go but up toward healing and being whole once more. You perhaps went to the doctor, acupuncturist, energy healing practitioner, nutritionist, etc. to assist you in the healing process. Then up you came, perhaps a little set back and then *whoosh*, back to a healthy you once more. During that adventure, you were forced to focus more on you to allow the healing to take place. You loved yourself a bit more and honored what you needed in the form of rest, nutrition, and medicine, if needed.

It has been long acknowledged that each human body has multiple energetic layers: physical, mental, emotional, and spiritual. The physical: what you see in the mirror. The mental: what you dwell upon, think about, and learn. The emotional: how you act/react to all situations. The spiritual: your God connection. Each layer contributes to who you are. Each layer is separate, but mingles with the other layers contributing to your personality, health, mindsets, and belief systems. These combined layers contribute to your aura, another tool that offers insights. However, ultimately, your aura is all about your soul in its current incarnation.

As an example, think of a time when you were very, very angry. This anger consumed you. You knew it was governing everything you did and how you acted (physical). You thought about it, contributing to it as it consumed you more (mental). You may have even felt sick over it, resulting in an upset stomach or headache (emotional). During the anger phase, forgiveness or love was just *not* an option (spiritual). This is just one example of how one emotion can and does hit all those various layers.

Raphael's Compass Direction

Raphael's direction is east. The direction of east symbolizes new beginnings, just like the beginning of a new day when the sun rises. The element association with east is Air. If you have ever witnessed a sunrise, you may remember the wind gently kicking up a few notches as the sun breaks free of the horizon.

Raphael's Chakra Association

Raphael oversees the heart chakra, and its location is obvious: the region of the heart. The heart chakra's color is green, which, of course, is also the color associated with Raphael. Envision an emerald with a light behind it. This light illuminates the emerald for all the universe to see its inner beauty. What a beautiful metaphor for you; be true to your heart and you shall shine!

The heart is the birthplace of your soul. Since your soul knows all, it never lies. It dances energetically and specifically to the musical note of F, as in, you have a very *F*ull heart; so full that there is more than enough to give to another without a thought of what is in it for you. When your heart chakra is out of alignment, you can become codependent, uncaring, greedy, callous, calculating, overly sentimental, and have fears of betrayal.

Here's a tidbit that may make you chuckle about your heart chakra: it doesn't matter whether you are standing on your feet or your head, the heart stays in the center! Your heart is the birthplace of your soul; therefore, it knows the truth. If ever in a quandary about something, place your hand over your soul center, over your heart, and listen to its loving wisdom.

Angelic Activity

Before you get hung up on the idea of forgiving something so horrific . . . keep in mind that it is only through true forgiveness that healing can take place. Remember, forgiving does not mean forgetting. When one for*gives*, one gives life back to themselves. It means that you have experienced the adventure and have no desire to experience it again and are ready to move on. If you hold on to the hurt and the anger, the angst wins by controlling you in ways unknown. The other person? They are going on their merry way without a thought in the world. It is akin to you taking poison and hoping they get sick. They really don't care. You are doing a disservice to yourself and can become stagnant and paralyzed with life. Make for*giving* part of your daily regime.

One beautiful, profound, and loving healing modality is the ancient Hawaiian healing practice called Ho'oponopono. Its basic premise is that you are responsible for all that is introduced (not necessarily experienced directly) into your world. In other words, there is an aspect within you that has caused it to be presented. By focusing on the event, notice where it seems to settle within your body energetically. Then repeat this loving phrase:

I'm sorry,
Please forgive me.
I love you,
Thank you.

The results are beyond profound.

Raphael's Healing Crystals

As you are probably by now figuring out, each angel can have many crystals that assist in enhancing their energies in the here and now. For the purpose of this book, the emerald and green calcite crystals are recommended when chatting with Raphael.

Emerald, because it is known for abundant love, is perhaps one of the reasons it is May's birthstone and is often used in engagement rings (yes, diamonds, watch out, emerald is here!). It can assist by helping to dispel negative mindsets, allowing positive actions and outcomes to occur. Emerald can also inspire one to search for the truth and meaning of any situation. This is in perfect alignment with Raphael's mission to help you find love of self, search for those deeply hidden issues, and allow them to be healed through love.

Green calcite is known to assist in improving overall health and well-being while enhancing the vitality of all the organs in the heart region, including the thymus and lower lungs. It is also a soothing stone to assist those wishing to conquer any addiction or compulsive disorder. On the non health side, green calcite is associated with manifesting monetary wealth and dispelling negative thought patterns.

Angelic Aromatherapy

Rose Otto: opens your heart chakra, bringing in love, inner peace, and compassion.

Palmarosa: helps relax your muscles, calms the mind, and invigorates the soul.

Thyme and Juniper: both very cleansing and refreshing in their energies.

Blue Green Algae Extract: while this may sound odd, this extract can be eaten, as it is high in superfoods, vitamins, and antioxidants.

Raphael's Askfirmations

Why is it so easy for me to connect with Archangel Raphael?

Why is it so easy for me to heal?

Why is it so easy to strengthen my connection with my guardian angel?
Why am I worthy of the love I desire?

Raphael's Fun Fact:

His animal association is the monkey. Why? Monkeys are the closest mammal to *Homo sapiens*. They are a prime example of living in the moment, allowing self to experience all life has to offer, including, you got it, healing.

Guided Meditation with Archangel Raphael

Sit facing east.

Breathe in,
Hold for four counts,
Breathe out.

Call on Archangel Michael and his legions,
To stand guard while you meditate.

Breathe in,
Hold for four counts,
Breathe out.

The room fills.
It gets warmer,
As Michael and his legions enter to stand guard,
During this meditation.

Breathe in,
Hold for four counts,
Breathe out.

It is now time to call on,
Archangel Raphael.

Breathe in,
Hold for four counts,
Breathe out.

The energy of the room settles in.
It feels more at peace.
It feels more loving.
It opens you to healing.

Breathe in,
Hold for four counts,
Breathe out.

As Raphael enters,
You relax more.

Breathe in,
Hold for four counts,
Breathe out.

You know it is time,
Time to heal,
Anything and everything that is ready.

Breathe in,
Hold for four counts,
Breathe out.

As Raphael comes closer still,
You share with him,
What you would like to heal now.

Breathe in,
Hold for four counts,
Breathe out.

You also share that you are open to healing,
Anything and everything else,
That you are not aware of at the present time.

Breathe in,
Hold for four counts,
Breathe out.

Raphael asks that you rest your hands,
With palms facing up.

Breathe in,
Hold for four counts,
Breathe out.

You feel a palm, a presence, an energy,
Resting on the top of your head.

Breathe in,
Hold for four counts,
Breathe out.

A warmth cascades over your entire being.

Breathe in,
Hold for four counts,
Breathe out.

Repeat.

Breathe in,
Hold for four counts,
Breathe out.

As you continue breathing,
Raphael pours some healing salve onto his fingertips.

Breathe in,
Hold for four counts,
Breathe out.

He starts by anointing your hands,
So you may feel alive once more.

Breathe in,
Hold for four counts,
Breathe out.

He then ministers to your eyes,
Allowing you to see only love and truth.

Breathe in,
Hold for four counts,
Breathe out.

He then dabs each ear,
So you may only hear the love you deserve,
And the truth of all.

Breathe in,
Hold for four counts,
Breathe out.

Raphael then dabs a bit on each side of your nose,
Allowing you to smell the sweetness of life.

Breathe in,
Hold for four counts,
Breathe out.

Raphael then lightly touches your lips,
Allowing you to taste the goodness that life offers.

Breathe in,
Hold for four counts,
Breathe out.

Now, continue breathing,
As Raphael addresses your specific concerns.

Breathe in,
Hold for four counts,
Breathe out.

Softly, slowly.

Breathe in,
Hold for four counts,
Breathe out.

You relax more deeply.

Breathe in,
Hold for four counts,
Breathe out.

Raphael shares with you,
Bits of information that will help the healing continue,
After this meditation is over.

Breathe in,
Hold for four counts,
Breathe out.

He also reminds you to rest easy,
Drink water,
And be gentle on yourself.

Breathe in,
Hold for four counts,
Breathe out.

Raise your hands to your heart.

Breathe in,
Hold for four counts,
Breathe out.

Raphael infuses you once more,
With a gentle blast of loving healing.

Breathe in,
Hold for four counts,
Breathe out.

His energy begins to pull back,
Gently,
Softly.

Breathe in,
Hold for four counts,
Breathe out.

The room surrounding you becomes more alive.

Breathe in,
Hold for four counts,
Breathe out.

You wiggle your hands and toes.

Breathe in,
Hold for four counts,
Breathe out.

Your body stretches.

Breathe in,
Hold for four counts,
Breathe out.

You smile,
You feel refreshed,
Your eyes open fully.

Breathe in,
Hold for four counts,
Breathe out.

Once more.

Breathe in,
Hold for four counts,
Breathe out.

7

Archangel Chamuel

Angel of Self-Love

"Love has no conditions. Love is pure. Love is all. Love yourself first."
—Archangel Chamuel

Archangel Chamuel is frequently confused with angels Samael, Shamael, and Kamael. This is probably due to the fact that the names sound and are spelled similarly. However, they are indeed separate from each other.

Chamuel greatly assists in the areas of dissolving negative emotions and thought patterns; especially toward self. She dissolves the self-deprecating patterns of not being good enough or not standing on one's own merit. Part of what gets dissolved is compulsive behavior. Shopping, gambling, eating; each of these can fall under the auspices of self-destruction, putting the responsibility on something (or someone) else to make one happy versus finding that inner happiness and allowing it to blossom into a true love affair with self. However, it must be noted that putting yourself first *is* considered selfish! Not in an ego-centric way, but in a very loving sort of way. You realize that because you are loving yourself first from a deeper place, you have more to offer to the universe.

As you are beginning to grasp, Chamuel is about the relationship with self. What does your relationship with yourself tell the world? You may not have servants to dress, bathe, and adorn you, but that is no reason not to tend to yourself as if there were. Take time daily to love your body as you bathe, dress, and go about your day. Thank each part of it for carrying you as you walk through life. Thank those smile wrinkles; it means much joy has entered your life. Eat foods that truly nourish as well as taste great. Exercise in ways that make you feel good. Meditate to fulfill the spiritual soul.

In other words, if you are not honoring yourself enough, why would anyone else do it for you? This is what Chamuel helps you to do—put yourself first. Put it this way, when you tend to *you*, the world at large takes note. You might as well wear a sign that says:

Hey, I'm taking care of me!

Hey, I'm important!

Therefore, I expect my needs, desires, and dreams to be actualized!

And it begins to happen. Chamuel is also instrumental in helping dissolve destructive behaviors, especially those directed at self. How often does one do nothing toward their dreams? Inertia = self-destruction. How often does one overeat, drink, or use drugs? Excess = self-destruction. How often does your thought process take over and is ultimately self-deprecating? Ick = self-destruction

Get the idea? It's not pretty, and it's high time *all of us* love ourselves more and give ourselves permission to achieve our desires. As an example, alcohol and drugs are easily recognized as destructive when not used appropriately and with respect. However, equally destructive is putting other's needs ahead of your own; stepping aside to allow others to constantly and consistently move forward while you simply smile and allow them to walk over you. It is certainly a beautiful thing to allow another in front of you at the checkout if you have a full cart and they look frazzled or have a disgruntled child, etc. It's another thing to allow it daily at the expense of your needs. The more the sense of self is diminished, the more the light from within you diminishes. This eventually leaves an empty shell where a glorious, radiant person once resided.

Zodiac Association

Chamuel connects with Taurus in the zodiac. Taurus, the bull? Yeppers! Taurus is well known to be stubborn, independent, and can break things up. While that might not sound very enticing, it is true to the energy and mission of

Chamuel. Being comfortable enough with self, loving self, and honoring self to know when to say *no* and mean it. When it is time to be alone and know it's okay. When it is time to be fully there because the bull has taken care of him or herself first, and can now can help another.

Chamuel's Name Defined

Archangel Chamuel's name, translated, means "he who sees God." Since you are a spiritual soul, within you is the God presence. Therefore, Chamuel's name could also mean "he/she who sees self." Seeing is recognizing. Recognition is a form of love. Interpreting Chamuel's name once again, it also could stand for "he/she who loves self."

Chamuel's Light Temple

Chamuel's light temple is located in St. Louis, Missouri. When we lived in that area, I loved to gaze up at the arch in downtown St. Louis and imagine her there. The arch would glisten in the light and periodically send out rays illuminating something on the ground. What would illuminate? Something that represented love; a family having fun, a feather, or periodically a rainbow. All would have me stop, smile, and breathe in the love energy that was ever-present. Each moment filled my heart to overflowing and I carried on with the day at hand with greater joy.

Chamuel's Symbol

Turn this page upside down and look at Chamuel's symbol. What do you see? Perhaps it reminds you of a heart that is open at the bottom. Turn it back around. Now what do you see? A heart that is open to receive all it desires and needs to not only function, but to thrive and blossom. When this knowledge begins to seep in and become embedded, such energy is empowering and can carry one through life through the power of love.

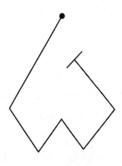

Chamuel's mission is not to better relationships in general, but to better the relationship one has with self.

Chamuel's Compass Direction

Archangel Chamuel's compass direction is southwest. The direction of southwest is about balance. To wrap it more in angelic knowledge, it is a reminder from Chamuel not to love another more than yourself. To not be of service so much that you become drained. To keep things in balance. Think of your beautiful heart like a pendulum; it swings back and forth, but will ultimately come back to center.

Chamuel's Chakra Association

Chamuel's chakra, like Raphael's, is the heart. The difference between the two is that Raphael, as you now know, is healing-based, while Chamuel is all about self-love. Loving self is, of course, incredibly healing; it simply takes a different trajectory.

Chamuel's color resonance is pink, pink, and more pink. If you are an artist, you know that the colors red and white make pink. When you look at those two colors energetically, it is the union of two rays: red, the physical ray, and white, the spiritual awakening ray. United, they create pink. Energetically, the physical joins with the spiritual, creating a union of feeling secure enough within self to pursue one's spiritual journey. Therefore, one can say with certainty that pink is the color of self-love. Through this power of love toward self, beauty, compassion, and trueness emerge. These traits emerge from within and softly radiate out to the world around you. When you step into your true love of self, you begin to realize that all is indeed possible. You don't have to boast about who you are and what you do. It simply is. You don't have to show off in any genre; money, house, spouse, clothing, career, jewelry, etc., it is what it is. You give and receive with pure aplomb. You can do so because you tend to you first, which allows the fountain to constantly flow; receive, give, receive, give. Notice the cadence, *receive*, then give, *receive*, then give. This simply cannot be stressed enough—one must *receive* in order to give freely.

When you love yourself first and foremost, loving others becomes easier. Judgment of others lessens because one recognizes that not one person is perfect and the imperfections witnessed are a testament to being human. Loving self-first builds self-esteem, confidence, and, yes, it is quite empowering. If we took this philosophy a step further, all that racial tension? Gone. Wars? They would become a thing of the past. All the angst at large would be gone as all enter and embrace that state called Christ consciousness. This is an energy state of being. Christ consciousness harkens to being one with *all*, not just a select few as you see fit. Tall order? Perhaps, but it all starts from within. It starts with you.

To offer a more mainstream example: have you ever flown on a commercial airplane? The flight attendants go through their safety lecture prior to takeoff. They remind you that if the air masks drop from the ceiling, "please put on your air mask before assisting another." They are right—help yourself first, then others can be helped. By tending to you first, you keep your glass full and, at times, overflowing. Having an overflowing vessel allows you to openly help others without doing so begrudgingly or without endangering your life. In other words, you can assist with a full heart (and in this case, full lungs).

You see, giving love is one thing, and is much easier for most to accomplish. Receiving love is a completely different animal. Receiving love when self-esteem or low self-worth is present can be a daunting task. Don't believe me? How often have you downplayed a compliment? How often have you shared where you got your outfit as a way to take the spotlight off of you? As another example, abundance is difficult to maintain when one feels defeated or not worthy. Chat with Chamuel more often to seamlessly receive those compliments and all that is desired with an open heart.

Another lesson in receiving love and loving self is learning to say *no*.

Repeat after me . . . *no*.

Saying no helps with boundaries. Not overextending and becoming a rubber band that gets s-t-r-e-t-c-h-e-d and eventually unable to snap back. Saying no when warranted can also be the end of another compulsive disorder: people pleaser. It's about creating boundaries for you and what you wish to be involved in.

Think of it this way, if you say yes to something, but really don't want to, you become drained. Perhaps irritable. Perhaps snarky. Resentment and anger can manifest inwardly and show themselves. Isn't there enough of that in the world already? By saying no, you are actually giving up space for someone else to participate who may truly enjoy being there. Just say no!

Angelic Activity

The following exercise was handed down by Chamuel to help you love *you* more. The rules are quite simple. Do not go to the next step until the current step you are on is done easily, effortlessly, and lovingly. You may always back up, but never jump ahead; you'll miss the fun of the journey.

Five Steps to "I Love You"

1. Place your hands over your heart. Listen to the cadence of its beat. Feel your chest rise and fall as you breathe. Call in the angels to gather and offer and give you love. Your only job? Receive. It's a beautiful way to go to sleep.

   Explanation of step one: your heart is the birthplace of your soul. By placing your hands there, you are recognizing you. Recognition is a form of love. Therefore, you are loving you.

2. Repeat step one, and add the phrase, "I love you." Your soul now hears these words and begins to soften and expand. Hold your hands in place for a minimum of three minutes and repeat, "I love you," as often as you desire.

   Explanation of step two: it takes receiving to yet another level and, by hearing these three little words, the body softens and the barrier of protection that is so often surrounding our bodies begins to crumble. Crumbling is a good thing. Really. That layer of protection now allows the goodness of the universe to empower you through love.

3. Repeat step two, and add your birth name. " _____, I Love You."

   Explanation of step three: our soul does not recognize any name other than the name given at birth. This includes terms of endearment, nicknames, or unsavory names. If you have legally changed your name, use that one. When the birth name is used, the soul is being recognized for its essence. As you now understand, recognition is a form of love.

4. Go to a mirror and look into those gorgeous, gorgeous eyes of yours. Place your hands over your heart and say, "I love you." Hold and look

into your insightful eyes, the window to your soul. Let the emotion of love wash over you and sink deep into your psyche.

Explanation of step four: by looking deep into your eyes, not at wrinkles, gray hairs, pimples, or any imperfections, you again are recognizing your soul.

5. Repeat step four. This is the cream of the crop, the pièce de résistance, so to speak, except you knew it was coming. Add your birth name. "_____, "I love you."

Explanation of step five: in this last step, you not only use your birth name, but address your soul through vision. You are seen, heard, and loved. This exercise is incredibly powerful in its love. Humans have made love so conditional we now feel the need to add the word unconditional in front to discern one from the other. There could be a book on just this very topic. This is how deep it runs and yet how powerful. Never do this. Love is love. Love *is* unconditional. Love is giving. Love is joy. Love is non judgmental. Love is purity at its finest. There are no conditions.

Chamuel's Healing Crystals

The prime crystal for Chamuel is rose quartz. Its energies of love are just what the angels ordered. It brings about a sense of non judgment while infusing its user with waves of love toward self. Rose quartz can be easily found and is quite affordable. This is just a small indication of how much the world truly needs love on all levels more than ever; especially toward self. If you are looking to enhance your current romantic partnership or to attract one, arrange two pieces of rose quartz in the shape of a heart to be placed on your love altar. If creating a romance or enhancing your current one, remember to get two of everything; you do not wish to be single (this is only one of something). Likewise, if you do not wish to attract an affair, no threes.

If you would like a crystal that resonates with both Chamuel and Raphael, look for watermelon tourmaline. It is ideal at cleansing and removing blockages. It is also known to assist in removing insecurities. Watermelon tourmaline is associated with calming overactive emotions, including compulsive behaviors. It is also energetically predisposed to help attract love and resolve issues in relationships, infusing them with joy and love. As you continue reading and better understanding the energies of Chamuel, you will see why this is a great combination; loving self from the inside first helps to heal all. Through that healing, you begin to live life more on your terms, not society's.

Angelic Aromatherapy

Rose Otto: opens your heart chakra, bringing in love, inner peace, and compassion toward self and others.

French Lavender: expands the essence of love.

Vanilla Bean: helps to relax the body and counteract any form of depression. This allows one to honor who they are in that moment. In essence, they can love themselves more.

Amber: is very similar to vanilla, in that it helps to alleviate depression while relaxing the brain waves and all that not-so-nice chatter the ego can throw at you.

Chamuel's Askfirmations

Why is it so easy for me to be selfish and take care of myself?

Why is it so easy for me to love me?

Why is it so easy for me to honor my needs?

Why is it so easy for me to give and receive love?

Chamuel's Fun Facts

★ Chamuel can help you find things when they seem to have gotten lost! Animals:

★ Deer because of their symbolic meaning of gentleness, kindness, and love.

★ Doves bring about peace, not only generally but feeling peace from within toward self.

★ Rabbits are similar to deer in that their energies are sweet, kind, loving, and very trusting.

★ Butterflies are widely accepted to be the symbol of transformation. When one loves themselves more, they simply transform and soar!

Guided Meditation with Archangel Chamuel

Sit facing southwest.

Breathe in,
Hold for four counts,
Breathe out.

Call on Archangel Michael and his legions,
To stand guard while you meditate.

Breathe in,
Hold for four counts,
Breathe out.

The room fills,
It gets warmer,
As Michael and his legion enter to stand guard,
during this meditation.

Breathe in,
Hold for four counts,
Breathe out.

It is now time to call on,
Archangel Chamuel.

Breathe in,
Hold for four counts,
Breathe out.

Chamuel enters softly,
Lovingly.
There may even be a hint of rose in the air.

Breathe in,
Hold for four counts,
Breathe out.

As she approaches,
You feel as though you are being hugged.

Breathe in,
Hold for four counts,
Breathe out.

You relax into this hug,
Feeling safe,
Loved,
At peace.

Breathe in,
Hold for four counts,
Breathe out.

Your entire being begins to relax.

Breathe in,
Hold for four counts,
Breathe out.

You feel more nurtured.

Breathe in,
Hold for four counts,
Breathe out.

As this hug continues,
You feel your energy softly rise,
More powerful in its softness.

Breathe in,
Hold for four counts,
Breathe out.

You feel important,
For you are.

Breathe in,
Hold for four counts,
Breathe out.

Chamuel gently reminds you,
Of your inner beauty,
Your charms,
Your worthiness,
Your dreams that are so very important to manifest.

Breathe in,
Hold for four counts,
Breathe out.

Repeat.

Breathe in,
Hold for four counts,
Breathe out.

Chamuel gently places a wing over your heart,
Softly infusing you with the energy of love,
Love toward self.

Breathe in,
Hold for four counts,
Breathe out.

Your heart expands,
Glows,
Receives.

Breathe in,
Hold for four counts,
Breathe out.

You find yourself,
Smiling,
Relaxing,
Receiving love in all its glory.

Breathe in,
Hold for four counts,
Breathe out.

You now place your hands over your heart,
Feel the life,
The joy,
The love.

Breathe in,
Hold for four counts,
Breathe out.

Continue breathing,
And receiving.

Breathe in,
Hold for four counts,
Breathe out.

Continue breathing,
And receiving.

Breathe in,
Hold for four counts,
Breathe out.

It is time for this session to come to a close.

Breathe in,
Hold for four counts,
Breathe out.

Chamuel begins to pulls away,
But the love remains.

Breathe in,
Hold for four counts,
Breathe out.

The room and its noises,
Begin to ground you.

Breathe in,
Hold for four counts,
Breathe out.

You feel your body once more.

Breathe in,
Hold for four counts,
Breathe out.

You inhale deeply and exhale loudly.
Welcome back.

8

Archangel Haniel (The Manifester)

Angel of Manifestation

"You are deserving of all that you desire. Never doubt it, not even for a moment."

—Archangel Haniel

Haniel is your go-to angel for many physical ailments. Ailments such as weight problems, fatigue, and diabetes. All three of these can be and are medically connected. Folks who are overweight tire easily and are more prone to be diabetic. In a more abstract sense, their sense of vibrancy in connection to life can become dull. Their expectancy of what life offers can become very tainted with feelings of *meh*, leading them to draw further into disconnection, perhaps with excess video gaming, TV watching, etc. At this juncture, revisit and reconnect with not only Haniel, but also Raphael and Chamuel. It's all about allowing self to receive love and to give permission to have the truest essence of you to emerge permanently.

From the spiritual viewpoint, Haniel helps widen your spiritual horizons. Think about it, if you are feeling more secure with yourself, you become more grounded. When you are more grounded, like that giant sequoia tree, you have deep roots that allow you to spread your wings and see all with great clarity. Once you are more grounded, you are able to see each drama for what it truly is: a life adventure. You can see why the cast of characters in your life are acting the way they do, what lessons are being studied, and the many possible solutions.

How cool is that?

Think of when you feel restricted. Ask Haniel to widen your horizons. Intuitive hits not hitting? Channels clogged? This is all Haniel's forte; time to chat away.

Haniel can also assist in situations when you feel nervous, such as giving speeches, meeting new people, and/or simply being human and not always fitting in (there's a bit of Uriel in this one, being safe to be you—see how the chakras support each other?). The range is that vast. Call on Haniel. I wish I had known more about him as a child. I fell into that last category and didn't really fit in. I found myself regularly checking that metaphorical watch and saying, "Oh my, look at the time, gotta go!" Go, of course, meant home, aka heaven.

I had an idyllic childhood, so I always felt safe at home, but I had trouble fitting in the confines of the physical body and being able to express myself clearly to others about what I saw, felt, sensed, etc. Initially I assumed (never assume anything, by the way) that all had this trait. However, as time went on, I realized that many could not do this, so I was considered weird and often overlooked. As a result of not knowing what the deal was and not feeling safe and certainly feeling like the oddball out, I got into the bad habit of fluttering my eyes. My parents had me medically tested to make sure there was nothing wrong. There wasn't, but the eyes continued. I realized that when my eyes fluttered, I was literally going outside of my body. Good thing I had a physical form, or I think I would have floated away. It wasn't until I understood why I was doing the "eye thing" that I started to come back and stay in my body.

As I came to understand this, I chatted with Haniel, did Askfirmations, and got clarity into who and what I am. As the knowledge sank in, my nervousness slowed down considerably. It didn't come to a screeching halt, but slowed *way* down. I can now look you square in the eye and share who I am, what I do, and what I'm here to do.

Thank you, Haniel.

Zodiac Association

Haniel connects with the zodiac sign, Aquarius. Aquarians are known to be very truthful. This is because they can speak more from the heart than most. They feel deeply and profoundly, and through those beautiful energies can become addicted to a variety of non empowering things. This is due to their sensitivity that can make it difficult to function in the here and now. I would wager a gander that a lot of Aquarians are also empaths. They feel from the heart and feel all. Haniel oversees this lovely group of souls to remind them of their sensitivity. He encourages them to embrace new ways to not only protect one from the unsavory, but to deal with it all in a more productive manner.

Haniel's Name Defined

Haniel's name, translated, means "Glory of God." What better angel to help create your heavenly desires here on Earth? Remember from the last chapter and Chamuel's name interpretation, you love self, see God in self, and therefore only create what you wholeheartedly desire (versus what your ego desires). Now, with a better understanding of Haniel, and with his tutelage, you are well on your way to live that life.

Angelic Encounter

Haniel has become such an instrumental part of my existence, as are the rest of The Gang, it's hard to pinpoint a chance or knowing encounter with him. So, I asked him, when was the first time you approached me?

Haniel reminded me of the first time I taught Reiki. I was a wreck and kept myself very, very busy in the kitchen the morning of. Doing things that didn't really need to get done, but kept my mind occupied. As I was putting away more dishes, a symbol showed itself to me that looked like a figure eight on its side with a line underneath.

"What's this?" I asked.

"The Symbol for Infinite Love. As you teach your new students today, infuse this symbol into their being. Remind them gently that love is infinite. Love has no boundaries. Love is complete."

Okay, then! Who am I to argue with that? Funny thing, as soon as our conversation was over, I felt renewed. I felt confident. I felt secure and scampered off to teach my first of many Reiki trainings.

Haniel's Light Temple

Haniel's light temple is located in Tibet. Tibet, of course, being the birthplace of His Holiness the Dalai Lama, who symbolizes peace and love and seeks to create a heaven on earth reality for all. Don't cha love it when the woo-woo is supported by the physical? Me too.

Haniel's Symbol

Haniel's symbol, like Chamuel, is reminiscent of a heart. In addition, his has the nod of the symbol vesica piscis. Now, compare it to Haniel's symbol.

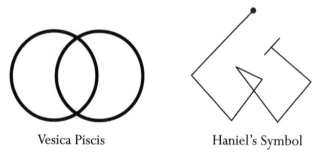

Vesica Piscis   Haniel's Symbol

See the similarities? If you look at the vesica piscis symbol, doesn't it slightly remind you of two wedding rings? Each coming together in sacred union. Each participating fully in the relationship to make it one. Each allowing the other their own individuality so they stay true to themselves. This is a bit of what Haniel can help you do; maintain your individuality to help you create your own heaven on earth reality. In other words, you live life on no one else's terms but your own.

Haniel's Compass Direction

Haniel's compass direction is southeast. Southeast represents not only new beginnings (east), but the fire energy to help fuel the flames of your soul's desire.

Haniel's Chakra Association

Beautiful Archangel Haniel oversees the etheric heart chakra. You may know this as the witness point, or high heart chakra, or thymus chakra. The angels provided me with the title etheric heart several years before hearing of the others. It rings truer because the etheric heart is the gateway, the opening of the union of heaven and earth. This union within the body symbolizes the heaven on earth existence that many yearn for. The etheric heart (heaven) and physical heart (earth) join together to create pure yumminess!

When your etheric heart chakra is in balance, the connection to the universe is strengthened and all is possible. Pure love for all is prevalent and is the underlying force from within. You become a manifesting magnet. You attract folks who get you, and without much explaining, a union of profound level is born. However, when your etheric heart chakra is out of balance, the disconnect to the heavens is prevalent and the woe-is-me syndrome can kick in. It becomes difficult, at best, to manifest any desire. Your desires can continue to seem like pipe dreams and you unknowingly embrace the mantra just-not-meant-to-be in an effort to ease the pain.

Angelic Activity

Using your newfound knowledge about the sacred symbol, vesica piscis, let's play! Draw two circles that overlap. One circle is you; it doesn't really matter which one you have chosen. Let's say you wish to lose weight, or you wish to have more clarity on your relationship with a special or not so special someone. Pick either of these scenarios to start and get comfortable with this process. Let's use food as an example. Do you allow food to fill a void (besides a grumbling stomach?) or do you eat predominantly for nourishment? What kinds of foods do you eat? What are your eating patterns? (Stress-based? Boredom-based? Hunger-based? Socially-based?) When you begin to notice what and why you eat, the relationship you have with food begins to change.

The same can be true for any personal relationship. Do you allow another person to control your life? Are you respected and listened to, or are you frequently talked over? Do you live your life around their schedule, needs, desires, and more, or is your relationship balanced, each contributing to the relationship equally?

The first step into this kind of play can appear daunting and time-consuming. Honestly, you may wish to fudge the truth once it shows itself, but remember that knowledge is power, and better understanding the behind-the-scenes energy for any scenario in your life can be liberating beyond your wildest dreams! I promise that, with practice, this activity becomes so easy to see and understand you will no longer need pen and paper!

Please give it a whirl; you deserve life on your terms.

Haniel's Healing Crystal

The crystal of choice for the etheric heart is turquoise. Turquoise is not only the birthstone for those born in the month of December, it is also a very high-resonating stone that truly emulates the spiritual and loving energies of this chakra. Helping to remind you that you are an aspect of the divine, this crystal can help eliminate the phenomena of self-sabotage that prevents you from living your heaven on earth existence. Turquoise also assists in the release of toxic buildup within the physical body, allowing one to ask and receive what is desired with greater clarity. It is associated with wealth, allowing one to accumulate wealth in all arenas of life: joy, love, monetarily, etc. Lastly, turquoise is known to balance the feminine and masculine aspects that each of us carries within us. Left side being feminine, right side being masculine; giving and receiving respectively.

Angelic Aromatherapy

Ylang-ylang: one of Haniel's go-to scents for many reasons; it helps boost heart rates (in a good way). It is also associated with being beneficial in treating insomnia and chronic fatigue, those physical maladies that can keep you from being proactive in creating your heavenly desires. Did you also know it is one of the ingredients in Chanel No. 5 perfume? True!

Jasmine (a personal favorite): this highly sought after aroma is known to uplift one's mood; in essence, getting excited about life once more!

Clary Sage: a lovely grounding oil that is known to relax and soothe the senses. Another great reminder to relax into your dreams to better allow them to manifest.

Coriander: known to stimulate the senses, including your creativity and optimism. Not to mention it is highly sought after for medicinal purposes.

Haniel's Askfirmations

Why is it so easy for me to speak my divine truth?

Why is it so easy to create my heaven on earth existence?

Why am I calm in all situations?

Haniel's Fun Facts

One of Haniel's animals is the leopard. There is an old saying, "The leopard never changes its spots." In this case, it's a beautiful thing; you come back to *you*. Shining only your essence, your beauty, your truth, your spots.

The other is the swallow. It mates for life (creating your perfect love affair) and is long known to be associated with nobility and intuition. Receiving wisdom from your ancestors long-passed, including the angels and ascended masters.

Guided Meditation with Archangel Haniel

Sit facing southeast.

Breathe in,
Hold for four counts,
Breathe out.

Call on Archangel Michael and his legions,
To stand guard while you meditate.

Breathe in,
Hold for four counts,
Breathe out.

The room fills.
It gets warmer,
As Michael and his legion enter to stand guard,
During this meditation.

Breathe in,
Hold for four counts,
Breathe out.

It is now time to call on,
Archangel Haniel.

Breathe in,
Hold for four counts,
Breathe out.

Haniel is here today,
To strengthen the relationship.
With your heart chakra,
And etheric heart chakra.

Breathe in,
Hold for four counts,
Breathe out.

As you place your hands,
Over your heart, you feel it beating stronger,
And it feels as though a door is opening.

Breathe in,
Hold for four counts,
Breathe out.

You begin to feel an opening at the top of your heart.

Breathe in,
Hold for four counts,
Breathe out.

As your heart begins to open,
A merging of love seeps in.
This love reminds you of what is important to you.

Breathe in,
Hold for four counts,
Breathe out.

Your desires are important.
Your health is important.
Your wisdom is important.
Your joy is important.

Breathe in,
Hold for four counts,
Breathe out.

Repeat.

Breathe in,
Hold for four counts,
Breathe out.

As your soul reminds you of what matters to you,
Embrace the knowledge,
Embrace the love,
Embrace the joy,
Embrace the manifestation.

Breathe in,
Hold for four counts,
Breathe out.

As Haniel enters more fully,
He reminds you of your worth,
Your greatness,
Your very essence.

Breathe in,
Hold for four counts,
Breathe out.

Haniel reminds you that you can create,
Your heaven on earth existence,
With great ease,
And from this moment forward, will work with you,
To create all.

Breathe in,
Hold for four counts,
Breathe out.

Repeat.

Breathe in,
Hold for four counts,
Breathe out.

Repeat.

Breathe in,
Hold for four counts,
Breathe out.

Sit with this powerful knowing and love for as long as necessary.

Breathe in,
Hold for four counts,
Breathe out.

Breathe in,
Hold for four counts,
Breathe out.

Breathe in,
Hold for four counts,
Breathe out.

As Haniel prepares to leave for now to close out this meditation,
He leaves you with the profound knowing that,
You have the power to create,
Your heaven on earth existence.

Breathe in,
Hold for four counts,
Breathe out.

The room and its noises,
Begin to ground you.

Breathe in,
Hold for four counts,
Breathe out.

You feel your body once more.

Breathe in,
Hold for four counts,
Breathe out.

You wiggle your toes and hands.

Breathe in,
Hold for four counts,
Breathe out.

You slowly open your eyes.

Breathe in,
Hold for four counts,
Breathe out.

You inhale deeply and exhale loudly.
Welcome back.

9

Archangel Raziel

Angel of Intuition

"Everything happens in divine timing. *You* are the divine, so all happens when *you* are ready."

—Archangel Raziel

One of the many beautiful attributes of Raziel and his specialty is that he shares glimpses of God which simply allow you to *be*. Think of those days when you simply went with the flow of life. You probably got more done because you weren't thinking of what should be done or not done next. You stayed in the moment of *now* and allowed life to unfold in its divine timing, ultimately becoming very connected and open to all of your intuitive blessings.

Raziel is associated with ancient wisdom. He is credited with writing the first book, the *Book of Raziel*, which is said to hold the secrets of the universe. He proclaims these secrets daily on Mt. Horeb, but as all things angelic, do not expect to drive there and see an angel making proclamations; Mt. Horeb is all energy. You may be very familiar with Mt. Horeb; it is the place where Moses was said to receive the Ten Commandments. Yes, you may know this sacred place as Mt. Sinai, and you would be correct. Both have become synonymous with the same location and event. Some have gone so far as to divide the mountain into two; eastern being Mt. Sinai and western being Mt. Horeb.

Because Raziel assists with enhancing intuitive gifts, he oversees the "Clairs." Clair is defined as clear, and represents the many ways intuition is given and received. When you digest the various clair definitions that follow, you will begin to see more clearly (pun intended) and understand your personal strengths.

Clairaudience (hearing). The better to hear you with, my dear. Those that have this gift can literally hear the messages, just like you would hear someone via a phone call.

Clairvoyance (seeing). Those with this gift can literally see. Just as you can see this book, a plate of food, or a flower, those with the sight can also see within their mind's eye. It is akin to a movie going on within the third eye area. Others may see on a different plane/dimension. All would fall under the category of clairvoyance.

Clairsentience (feeling). Some intuitionists who are more empathic can literally feel another's emotion, illness, angst, as well as their joys. Their feelings can offer insight into which chakra is currently off-kilter and can predict a source of an illness or where an illness has manifested. Those that are empathic would also be considered clairsentient. Think of the old saying "I have a gut feeling." This falls under the auspices of clairsentience. Empaths would certainly be considered heightened clairsentients.

Clairalience (smelling). This is a more obscure gift, but a gift, nonetheless. Some can garner insights on a variety of messages based on what they smell. They may smell food as a way to connect a client with a loved one who has skipped over. My grandmother and Mother Mary periodically make themselves known to me with the scent of roses. This is especially powerful when there are no roses in our home at the time!

Claircognizance (knowing). This one has you owning the title of little-miss- or little-mister-know-it-all. You simply know things. You can't explain why; you just do.

Clairgustance (tasting). No judgement here, but this is probably the most unusual of them all. Having said that, I have read cases of missing people where the intuitive was able to help locate them based on the gift of taste. Taste can be beneficial in the assistance of recalling information as well as predicting future situations.

Everyone has the ability to tap into and experience all six clairs listed above. But, just as we may be able to add 2+2, this does not make us all chemical engineers, right? You may be able to bake a cake, but are you running a patisserie? In other words, yes, you have intuitive prowess, but you may not be gifted in all categories. Most aren't; in fact, I would go so far as to say many aren't. It would be the rare person indeed to have equal standing with all the clairs.

For example, my strength is knowing: claircognizance. I'm a little-miss-know-it-all. However, when the angels really wish to get my attention and want to make sure the message will be received, another method of clair, such as scent or hearing, will emerge.

I'm sure the same goes for you. Can you recollect a time that something was so out of the ordinary for you that you paid attention and got a sign that made perfect sense? Whether it made sense immediately or made sense upon reflection.

As mentioned, Raziel is given credit for writing the first book, the *Book of Raziel*. Within the book lies magic and secret knowledge relating to the zodiac, protective spells, terrestrial knowledge, the names of God, as well as various healing methods. The book is known to be filled with metaphors, riddles, codes, etc. for life and humanity. Therefore, only those who are ready will understand its true meaning. The codes within the book are said to be the answers to humankind's DNA. The first coding created the tree of life, also called the gnostic tree of life; the basis of the Kabbalah, the study of life and how it functions on all levels.

It is also said that Raziel's book was given to Adam and Eve after they were expelled from the Garden of Eden to help them find their way back home. There is speculation that the book has journeyed to many; Noah, who imparted wisdom so he could build the ark, Enoch (who later became Metatron), and most recently it is said to have been in the possession of King Solomon.

Zodiac Association

Raziel is associated with Scorpio. Scorpios tend to be tenacious, passionate about all, and can see clearly the road ahead of them. But watch out for their sting! In that sting lies the truth. They intuitively know when something is false. This, of course, is provided that one is *listening* to their beautiful intuition! That is certainly where the energy of Raziel enters; helping one pay attention to their glorious intuition!

Raziel's Name Defined

Archangel Raziel's name is interpreted to mean "secrets of God." Once again, what a perfect insight into Raziel's area of expertise: intuition. Through the use of your great intuition, the secrets of God and the universe can be revealed. It is in the stillness of all that it comes forward. Never rushed, forced, or even wished upon. In the stillness, truth is found. Raziel oversees the third eye chakra; long believed to be the place of intuition, the place where we can obtain knowledge from the unknown and unleash the mysteries of the universe, and, of course, God.

Angelic Encounter

My angelic encounter actually indirectly involves me, through my mom. It was so profound, it has stayed with me for decades: my mom was driving along a country road near where we lived in Connecticut. The only folks in the car were her and my infant brother; this is an important fact, so stay with me. She passed a car and began to daydream, as we often can while traversing common roads. She was driving along, singing to herself and my brother and not necessarily paying attention to her surroundings, until very clearly and distinctly she heard the words, *move over now*. Without a second thought, she returned to her proper lane. Within moments, a car raced by her that surely would have caused a head-on collision. Who knows what those results may have been? We only know that we are thrilled mom listened and I have a baby brother and sister (who came later). All because a message was delivered quickly, fiercely, and received with great love.

Raziel's Light Temple

As the Angelic Secret Keeper, Raziel stands on Mt. Horeb daily to proclaim the secrets of men to all mankind. Relax your mind to softly hear this daily proclamation. As mentioned earlier, Mt. Horeb is also known as Mt. Sinai, the same place where Moses received the Ten Commandments. Ironically, Horeb is translated to mean "glowing heat," which can refer to the sun, while Sinai is derived from the name of Sin, the Sumerian deity of the moon. When you combine the two together, you have the sun and the moon. A beautiful balance, yet again. You might surmise that Raziel's light temple would be on Mt. Horeb. This would be a lovely educated guess, but not correct. It's actually in the middle of the Pacific Ocean where Lemuria once stood above the waters.

If you are unfamiliar with Lemuria, it is sometimes referred to as the lost continent of Mu in the time before Atlantis, before ego and fear infiltrated and took over. As mentioned in Haniel's section, this is the time when even the chakra system was linked in the vesica piscis; true support for all. Lemuria was the time of true energy. Purity. Love. In present time, only a few spots remain above water that are associated with Lemuria; Easter Island, parts of Australia, the Pacific Islands, and Mt. Shasta in California.

Raziel's Symbol

It probably doesn't take much imagination to see a connection between Raziel's symbol and a labyrinth. That is exactly what Raziel's intention is; go within to retrieve 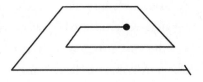 any and all information, but don't linger! One must venture out in order to share that information with the world at large. As with all, it's your intention that dictates what is received. However, at times, what is actually given can be even better than what we asked for! Don't dismay if your answers are not all that they seem. Allow the process to happen and enjoy the beautiful ride.

If you decide to meditate with Raziel's symbol, set your intention prior, just as you would with any other meditation, including a walk within a physical labyrinth. (Don't forget to call on Michael prior to starting!) Do you wish to bring information forward? Do you wish to dig deep to gain clarity on a situation? You may even place his symbol over your third eye for some added focused energy.

Raziel's Compass Direction

Raziel's direction of choice is southwest. I personally find this quite amusing as most, if not all, our homes have faced this direction. Southwest is a direction of great power, intensity, matriarchal energy, and now, Raziel.

Raziel's Chakra

Raziel's chakra association is the third eye. The location of the third eye chakra is smack dab in the middle of your forehead. You have probably seen illustrations depicting a third eye. Artists have purposefully created a third eye since recorded time, to illustrate that one must go within to find the answers.

Many on the spiritual path wish their third eye to be more open so they can see better. I call this be-careful-what-you-wish-for syndrome! So many have had their third eye pried open only to fervently wish it to close back up. There is more out there that you may not be able to imagine, comprehend, and/or handle. Allow yourself the journey to deepen and strengthen your intuitive abilities on your own schedule. You will get what you are ready to experience. Promise. If you suffer from headaches and the worst kind of headaches, migraines, you could be fighting the good fight; wanting to enhance your intuitive powers, but subconsciously pushing them away. Or just the opposite; not wishing to see the truth of any situation. If this is the case, meditate with Raziel and his symbol to allow yourself to be and feel safe in your intuitive prowess.

When your third eye is in balance, you simply go with the flow, messages are clear, and your discernment of who, what, and when is pristine and un-muddled. When your third eye chakra is off-kilter, ego steps in, feeding you with fear-based statements. This can make your intuition incorrect or, worse yet, not stated at all! The other side of this scenario can also offer illusions of grandeur, insecurities, etc. Headaches may become all too frequent when the third eye is out of balance. Other bodily ailments include high blood pressure and sinus issues. Raziel is also great at relieving back issues, such as sciatica, lumbago, or spinal pain, and is equally beneficial at easing bronchitis and insomnia. When one ignores their intuitive gifts, these ailments can ensue.

Angelic Activity

Experience Raziel's symbol for yourself as you go within to find the truth of any situation. Print out Raziel's symbol from the book. Have some paper and a writing implement close by. Call on Big Mike for protection.

Set your intention without being overly specific as to the outcome. If you are new to all of this, start with the basics, such as learning to trust your own intuitive powers. If you wish to take this deeper, perhaps explore any situation in your life that you would like greater clarity on.

Trace Raziel's symbol with a finger of your non dominant hand. Your dominant hand may become busy writing down information as you receive it.

Take your time with tracing. Remember, slow and steady wins the race. Slow and steady in this activity will help to slow your mind and expectations of what should happen versus what is the truth of the matter. As you traverse the symbol, jot down any images you receive. Jot down names, dates, phrases, etc. Initially it may seem very piecemeal, but oftentimes the puzzle pieces fit seamlessly together later.

Linger in the center of the symbol. Allow yourself to go a bit deeper as you ask your question once more. Ask for deeper clarity, if need be. When you are ready, use the same slow tempo as you unwind from the symbol, allowing you to process the information in the here and now.

Write down all information, whether you think it is pertinent or not. You may come back to it later and be quite surprised at its significance to the entire picture!

Raziel's Crystal

Raziel's crystal of choice is iolite. Iolite can help in many, many areas of your life.

★ It strengthens your spiritual gifts, as well as the heart/mind connection.
★ It gets the mind (ego) to relax to help you better understand your heart's (soul) urges with greater reverence.

★ It's instrumental in shamanic work while releasing those stored anger issues.

★ If you or someone you know who has an addiction (remember, addiction takes many forms, including soda, sex, drugs, cigarettes, sugar, etc.) iolite illuminates why this addiction is in place to help kick the habit once and for all.

★ It brings information forward that is connected to the Cathars, Knights of Templar, and Arthurian times.

★ It releases your mask to help your beautiful self shine.

★ It helps you accept responsibility; no more name-calling and finger-pointing.

★ It eliminates debt.

★ It blends the conscious with the intuitive.

Angelic Aromatherapy

Some of Raziel's scents of choice include:

Lemon Verbena: clears the path and illuminates the truth.

Patchouli: well known for bringing about a sense of sacredness to all things in life. As you take each step forward you are reminded that you are on a sacred path, no matter your vocation.

Rosemary: assists in rites of passage throughout life. This is one of the keys of Raziel, as each step within is a passage to incorporate into daily life.

Jasmine: opens consciousness to heavenly realms.

Narcissus: assists in inspiration and trance work.

Raziel's Askfirmations

Why is it so easy for me to trust my intuition?

Why is it so easy for me to understand my addiction to _____?

Why is life so bliss-filled?

Raziel's Fun Facts

★ Raziel is associated with other famous beings throughout spiritual history: Thoth, Herme, Merlin the magician, and Loki the trickster.

★ He is the patron angel of lawmakers and lawyers.

★ Raziel dances to the musical note of A, as in cl*air*, as in your vision is as clear as pure air.

Guided Meditation with Archangel Raziel

Sit facing southwest.

Breathe in,
Hold for four counts,
Breathe out.

Call on Archangel Michael and his legions,
To stand guard while you meditate.

Breathe in,
Hold for four counts,
Breathe out.

The room fills,
It gets warmer,
As Michael and his legion enter to stand guard,
During this meditation.

Breathe in,
Hold for four counts,
Breathe out.

It is now time to call on,
Archangel Raziel.

Breathe in,
Hold for four counts,
Breathe out.

Raziel enters from all directions.
Encasing you in wisdom from all sources.

Breathe in,
Hold for four counts,
Breathe out.

You may feel slight pressure on your third eye.

Breathe in,
Hold for four counts,
Breathe out.

As Raziel helps to gently,
Release your expectations of any outcome,
You relax into full trust mode.

Breathe in,
Hold for four counts,
Breathe out.

As your trust deepens,
So does your inner knowing.

Breathe in,
Hold for four counts,
Breathe out.

As your inner knowing deepens,
So does your acceptance.

Breathe in,
Hold for four counts,
Breathe out.

As your acceptance deepens,
So does your willingness,
To see and understand the truth of all.

Breathe in,
Hold for four counts,
Breathe out.

Embrace the truth.
The truth is liberating.
The truth is clear.
The truth is love.

Breathe in,
Hold for four counts,
Breathe out.

Repeat.

Breathe in,
Hold for four counts,
Breathe out.

Raziel gently kisses your third eye,
Leaving an imprint of love,
Clarity,
Wisdom,
Acceptance.

Breathe in,
Hold for four counts,
Breathe out.

His hands cup your ears,
To allow greater listening.

Breathe in,
Hold for four counts,
Breathe out.

Raziel touches your shoulders,
Allowing you to feel with a greater sense,
Of understanding and love.

Breathe in,
Hold for four counts,
Breathe out.

Raziel touches the tip of your nose,
To allow your sense of smell to become enhanced,
To enjoy the riches of life.

Breathe in,
Hold for four counts,
Breathe out.

Raziel covers your eyes,
And leaves behind the ability to see great love in all.

Breathe in,
Hold for four counts,
Breathe out.

Lastly, Raziel presses a finger to your mouth,
Allowing you to taste all the goodness that life has to offer.

Breathe in,
Hold for four counts,
Breathe out.

Repeat.

Breathe in,
Hold for four counts,
Breathe out.

As Raziel prepares to depart for the time being,
The room and its noises,
Begin to ground you.

Breathe in,
Hold for four counts,
Breathe out.

You feel your body once more.

Breathe in,
Hold for four counts,
Breathe out.

You wiggle your toes and hands.

Breathe in,
Hold for four counts,
Breathe out.

You slowly open your eyes.

Breathe in,
Hold for four counts,
Breathe out.

You inhale deeply and exhale loudly.
Welcome back.

10

Archangel Zadkiel

Angel of Sacred Space

"Shine ever brightly, my little one. The universe needs you now more than ever."

—Archangel Zadkiel

Zadkiel assists with the emotional side of life. When there are emotional issues simmering, it can be downright difficult to move forward in the rest of your life. If these issues are left unnoticed and disregarded, they can often propel one into addictions of all kinds: food, drugs, alcohol, gambling, sex, lying, etc.

On a spiritual level, Zadkiel can help enhance psychic abilities like past life regression. He also aids in meditation, which is perfect for those just starting out and not quite sure what to do. Chatting with Zadkiel will help ease your mind and allow you to reach the expansiveness sought out by meditation.

One can think of Zadkiel's violet flame as the violet flame of freedom, ridding yourself of all that is no longer serving you. Zadkiel will hold this sacred space until all can reach the ultimate goal to free themselves from self-created and self-inflicted negativity and limitations.

Zadkiel's sole mission is to clear away unwanted, lower, non positive energies, and turn them back to their original state of pureness. I personally use it daily to clear away unwanted baggage and cobwebs that are preventing me from doing what I'm here to do.

Zodiac Association

Zadkiel loves connecting with the Sagittarians of the world. Sagittarians have a very high BS monitor; they can tell when they are being fibbed to. This is in part because of Zadkiel's powers of transmutation. Like Zadkiel, Sagittarians don't fret over the little stuff. They can see the big picture in most situations, which greatly helps them soar through life and honor who they are and what they are here to do.

Zadkiel's Name Defined

Zadkiel's name translates to "righteousness of God." If one were to interpret this meaning, it could be something akin to allowing pureness to begin anew. Allowing you to begin anew. Giving yourself permission to simply be you. How cool is that?

Angelic Encounter

This encounter is definitely a bit more on the woo-woo part of things, so stick with me, for you can't deny the end result. I had a mentor years ago. As I got more comfortable in my power and gifts, she began to act unusual around me. She would do things, such as cut me off in conversation, act indifferent toward me, in general. This was very unlike her, initially. My ego immediately jumped in to say I had done something wrong. I must have insulted her in some way and more.

Of course, I had done nothing wrong; neither had she, so it was time to practice what I preach! I decided to meditate upon this matter with the help of Zadkiel. I went into a meditative state (but called on Big Mike first, obviously) and invited her to join me energetically. (Keep in mind that this was all through a meditation and not done while we sat together). After she energetically entered, we quickly began to morph to a life when we were part of an aboriginal tribe as brothers. She/he was the elder. According to tribal law, she/he was to succeed our father upon his death. The tribe did something unheard of, they voted to have me replace her/him instead! We had a conversation around the communal campfire. I explained that I did not campaign for this nor ask for it in any way. She/he began to understand. She/he knew he was not the best choice for the tribe and would ultimately lead them to war.

She/he knew that I was the more compassionate and forward thinking. We both shed tears of joy, love, and healing. We hugged each other. We left the campfire as brothers, and more importantly, friends once more.

The result in the present day? Magical. I shared the meditation with her. She was initially aghast that her actions had affected me so, but very intrigued about what had transpired. After that meeting, I don't believe we ever chatted much again; there was no need. We took an event that happened thousands of years ago and healed it. There was no need to connect further, for our karma was healed. To this day, she is still thought of fondly.

Zadkiel's Light Temple

Archangel Zadkiel works on the seventh ray, which is violet, and represents transmutation and purification. The seventh ray is also known as the violet/amethyst ray. It intensifies the powers of mercy, compassion, forgiveness, and freedom. The archangels of this ray share a retreat called the Temple of Purification that is located over Cuba. This is the location of Zadkiel's light temple. Just to further prove that once you open to receive the connection, all you see is *the* connection. As you will read momentarily, Zadkiel's chakra association is the crown chakra. Care to take a guess as to its color?

Zadkiel's Symbol

To allow all to walk their talk, Zadkiel's symbol demonstrates how humans can, at times, get easily distracted and go off course from their own passions and can still be brought back to center. Once back, they can stand strong from the ground up. This is illustrated as his symbol shoots off to the left, but then switches trajectory, coming gently back to center while still escalating. As each newfound piece of information is obtained, absorbed, and embraced, it drops into the core, the psyche, and is then assimilated into day-to-day life, allowing you to shine even more brightly.

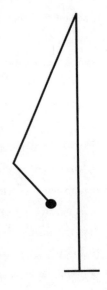

Put it this way: even when you get off track with life, you are never lost or so far gone to be considered a lost cause. By chatting with Zadkiel, you simply acknowledge that your current path is not serving you, and he will help you get back to your center and bring all that new and not-so-new information along with you. Bringing that information deeper into your psyche contributes to you shining brighter. Because it naturally embeds itself deeper, it becomes permanent, never to leave your side again. It becomes a natural part of your personality. In other words, you are better understanding all aspects of yourself with greater ease.

Think of these sidebar events as a life adventure; all contributing to your backpack of knowledge and experiences, thus molding you into your beautiful unique self. Is it any wonder that Zadkiel's areas of specialty are self-transformation, spiritual growth, and cosmic alchemy?

Zadkiel's Compass Direction

Zadkiel's compass direction is northeast. How poignant when considering the two directions independently; east represents new beginnings, and north equates to infinite possibilities. When you combine them, Zadkiel offers endless new beginnings. Therefore, Zadkiel's altar may hold your vision board. Put your intentions out into the universe and know that you can live the life you desire.

Zadkiel's Chakra Association

Zadkiel oversees the crown chakra. The very top of your head, the fontanelle; you know, that soft spot babies have when born. This chakra is resplendent violet (remember the light temple section?) and is represented by the 1,000-petal lotus that is called the Sahasrara. Its sole purpose is to help one detach from ego to reach nirvana and total spiritual evolution, ultimately allowing one to reach pure consciousness and ascend in their spiritual journey. Some of the great spiritual masters, such as Mahatma Gandhi and His Holiness the Dalai Llama, exude enlightenment while living a very human existence. They help others see the light within themselves and live more from the energy of love.

When your crown chakra is in balance, you are proactive in your self-realization and understand that we are all truly connected by a common source. It doesn't take much to realize how you are connected to someone, anyone in your life, and to feel, know, and embrace your true inner light.

When your crown chakra is unbalanced, you can be overly skeptical, caught up in the pursuit of spirituality (spiritual addiction) by taking endless classes, experiencing countless services without giving any one of them a chance to assimilate before jumping to the next. One may also suffer chronic exhaustion or depression. You also pray to the material gods. Materialism becomes your only source of enjoyment; the acquisition of the new best thing enhances your imaginary status.

Angelic Activity

Zadkiel is part of the trifecta, as I call them. The trifecta includes Michael, Raphael, and Zadkiel. These three are instrumental in the process of energy cord cutting. Energy cords are just what they sound like; cords of energy that connect you and another human. Any time you interact with another (the checkout line at the grocery store, a neighbor, a loved one, someone you pass on the street but catch their eye), a cord of energy is attached. Some energy cords are replenishing while others are draining.

The sole purpose of energy cord cutting is to bring your power back to you. When energy cords are cut, you stop feeling like pulled taffy and less drained. Think of cord cutting as an energetic loofa. Just as the physical loofa leaves your skin all sparkly, energized, and shiny, cord cutting does the same thing, but energetically.

As an example, you all have at least one person in your life that, when you think of them, you smile, feel those blessed, warm fuzzies, and more. These folks help fuel you through their love, joy, and support, no matter what.

On the other side of the coin are what is commonly referred to as psychic vampires. They don't even have to be in the room or the same building, but you can feel them draining you. You feel less than and tired just by thinking of them. You may have even used the phrase, "So-and-so is draining the life out of me."

The good news is that most are completely unaware that they are attached to you in this manner. It's an energetic phenomenon. Each person has many cords attached to them at any given moment. It's a natural thing, these energy cords, but you can take more control of your life by not allowing everyone to have a piece of you!

One thing worth noting prior to learning how to cut cords, is that cords of love can never be cut. Even if one has skipped back home (died), that cord can never be cut. Love is the strongest bond. However, if you and a loved one have a disagreement of some sort, it becomes a dis-cord. *That* cord can be cut and it is recommended that you do so. This allows the love to flow freely once again. I have been married for over thirty years (yes, thirty!). Over that time, we have had a disagreement or two; these are dis-cords. By having those cords cut, the love flows more freely between us, and our marriage? Stronger than ever.

Bottom line? You never have to worry about cutting a cord by accident.

Time to meet the trifecta:

Michael: the premier protector and cord cutter of the angelic realm. He can and does cut all cords that no longer serve you. Each cord is cut at both ends; you and the person it is attached to. Many of you who are familiar with cord cutting will already know this part.

Raphael: the healer of the angelic realm. Raphael swoops in right behind Michael and puts a healing salve over the energetic wounds of all parties concerned.

Zadkiel: the transmuter of the angelic realm. In other words, he turns each cord back to its original state of purity. This process is quite simple and is a lovely way to drift off to sleep at night.

Repeat these phrases:

Michael, thank you for cutting all cords that no longer serve me.
Raphael, thank you for healing all as each cord is cut.
Zadkiel, thank you for transmuting all cords.

That's it. Really. No overthinking allowed. As quickly as you can say it, it happens. For those that are curious, you may actually feel little pings as each cord is severed. However, I find the process so relaxing that I usually drift off to sleep.

Using the phrase "all cords that no longer serve me" is imperative. Do not go for the vampire cords or a cord you know you wish to be rid of. Those cords, no matter how long or short they have been attached, are powerful. They are pulling on your energy. Your body has gotten used to it and to have it cut prior to gaining your power back could leave you literally ill. To reinforce this philosophy, think of a time when you held it together for an extended period of time. Once the event was over, you most likely collapsed and may have even gotten sick. This is a similar kind of scenario. If you cut cords regularly, ideally, daily, by the time you get to the vampire cord, it will be just as insignificant as those other little ones that are getting cut now. Why? Because cutting your energy cords brings your power back to you and makes you stronger. Such an easy, empowering tool to implement, and potentially life-changing.

Zadkiel's Healing Crystal

If you have been paying attention, and I know you have, you ought not be surprised at Zadkiel's crystal choice: amethyst. Amethyst is the physical manifestation of the violet flame. One of amethyst's features is that it constantly transmutes energies of the space it's in. Now knowing that, doesn't it make perfect sense why so many spas, metaphysical centers, etc. have an amethyst in their waiting area or scattered throughout their place of business? The secret is out! Amethyst is doing one of the many things it naturally does; clearing the energy. It is why these places of business feel so welcoming and clear; because they are!

Angelic Aromatherapy

Zadkiel is associated with many essential oils, but one of my favorites is **juniper** for its purification and protective energies. It is also known to assist in clearing past traumas while dispelling negativity. **Clary sage** is another oil associated with Zadkiel. It helps in meditation by clearing away inner conflicts. I adore **frangipani oil** in connection to Zadkiel. Frangipani, also known as plumeria, is used to invoke love and spirituality.

Zadkiel's Askfirmations

Why is it so easy for me to allow transmutation in my world?
Why is it so easy for me to tend to me first?
Why can I be me?

Zadkiel's Fun Fact

Zadkiel's musical note is B, as in *b*irthing your right to live life on your terms.

Guided Meditation with Archangel Zadkiel

Sit facing northeast.

Breathe in for four counts,
Hold for four counts,
Breathe out for four counts,

Call on Archangel Michael and his legions,
To stand guard while you meditate.

Breathe in for four counts,
Hold for four counts,
Breathe out for four counts.

The room fills.
It gets warmer,
As Michael and his legion enter to stand guard,
During this meditation.

Breathe in for four counts,
Hold for four counts,
Breathe out for four counts.

It is now time to call on,
Archangel Zadkiel.

Breathe in for four counts,
Hold for four counts,
Breathe out for four counts.

As Zadkiel enters, a lightness fills the room,
Bringing with it a great sense of sacredness,
Clearing,
Clarity,
Truth.

Breathe in for four counts,
Hold for four counts,
Breathe out for four counts.

The energy continues to build,
And you rest in the comfort of angels' wings.
And allow the clearing to take place.

Breathe in for four counts,
Hold for four counts,
Breathe out for four counts.

As Zadkiel more fully enters,
He begins to pour the energy of the violet flame over you.

Breathe in for four counts,
Hold for four counts,
Breathe out for four counts.

The energy starts above your crown chakra.
It feels warm and tingling as it cleanses.

Breathe in for four counts,
Hold for four counts,
Breathe out for four counts.

The energy continues to be poured over you,
Gently cascading down your body,
Slowly, ever so slowly.

Breathe in for four counts,
Hold for four counts,
Breathe out for four counts.

It reaches deep into your ears,
Cleansing out old phrases and words,
That do not serve you.

Breathe in for four counts,
Hold for four counts,
Breathe out for four counts.

It cleanses your eyes,
Enabling you to see the truth in all.

Breathe in for four counts,
Hold for four counts,
Breathe out for four counts.

It reaches deep into your mouth,
Allowing you to speak your truth,
From the essence of love.

Breathe in for four counts,
Hold for four counts,
Breathe out for four counts.

As it reaches your shoulders,
The weight you've been carrying is lifted off.

Breathe in for four counts,
Hold for four counts,
Breathe out for four counts.

It continues downward,
And releases all tension surrounding your heart.

Breathe in for four counts,
Hold for four counts,
Breathe out for four counts.

The violet flame not only encases your physical body,
But reaches within to cleanse every organ.

Breathe in for four counts,
Hold for four counts,
Breathe out for four counts.

Feel it linger in areas that require and desire more.

Breathe in for four counts,
Hold for four counts,
Breathe out for four counts.

Continue breathing as the flame,
Cleanses the area around your hips,
Allowing you to move forward with more grace.

Breathe in for four counts,
Hold for four counts,
Breathe out for four counts.

It continues its journey south and cleanses your knees,
Allowing you to feel more flexibility and support.

Breathe in for four counts,
Hold for four counts,
Breathe out for four counts.

It ventures down to your feet,
And you now feel complete support,
Not only from self, but from the world at large.

Breathe in for four counts,
Hold for four counts,
Breathe out for four counts.

It lastly and fully encases you,
From below your feet to above your head.

Breathe in for four counts,
Hold for four counts,
Breathe out for four counts.

Repeat.

Breathe in for four counts,
Hold for four counts,
Breathe out for four counts.

Repeat.

Breathe in for four counts,
Hold for four counts,
Breathe out for four counts.

As Zadkiel begins to close today's session,
He reminds you,
That you can visit this as often as you desire.

Breathe in for four counts,
Hold for four counts,
Breathe out for four counts.

As Zadkiel prepares to depart for the time being,
The room and its noises,
Begin to ground you.

Breathe in for four counts,
Hold for four counts,
Breathe out for four counts.

You feel your body once more.

Breathe in for four counts,
Hold for four counts,
Breathe out for four counts.

You wiggle your toes and hands.

Breathe in for four counts,
Hold for four counts,
Breathe out for four counts.

You slowly open your eyes.

Breathe in for four counts,
Hold for four counts,
Breathe out for four counts.

You inhale deeply and exhale loudly.
Welcome back.

11

Archangel Metatron

Angel of Motivation

"Dearest one, I am forever by your side, helping to illuminate the very essence of your being to the universe at large."

—Archangel Metatron

It's almost difficult to know where to start when chatting about Metatron. He's quite the complex "guy." Metatron is not just an angel. He's not just an ascended master. For those unfamiliar with the term ascended master, allow me a brief moment to explain. An ascended master was a human who evolved to such levels of spirituality, they ascended into heaven. Think of Mahatma Gandhi, Buddha, Mother Mary, and Kwan Yin. These masters continue to serve humanity from their heavenly status and will continue to do so until all have ascended.

There is a hint within Metatron's name as to his status. Notice the ending, Metatron. All angel names that end in "-on" are accredited with being human prior to becoming an angel (Just like Metatron's twin, Sandalphon.).

Metatron has been in human form many times. Two of his known identities are Shah Jahan (the Shah who built the Taj Mahal) and more notably, Enoch, Noah's great-grandfather. As Enoch, he walked with God and was turned to flame, his eyelashes to flashes of lightning. God then placed him on the throne of glory and gave him the name Metatron. Unlike many tales of popular fiction, Metatron is *not* a fallen angel. Far from it, actually.

Metatron is all; as stated previously, not just an angel, not just an ascended master. He oversees all things physical within your body and helps restore vibrancy. He assists in balancing not just the physical aspects of the human body, but all mental, emotional, and spiritual aspects. As discussed in Raphael's chapter, all of these layers work together to create the whole. When one is off, it affects the others to varying degrees.

He oversees the Akashic Records and helps those who read the records tap into the correct file, as needed. The Akashic Records are also known as the Hall of Records. These records hold information of every lifetime for every single person; past, present, as well as future. Think of the largest library holding only soul patterns, karma, dharma, soul's mission, etc. What a library, indeed! He helps us keep life in perspective by making sure that as we give lovingly, we also remember to take care of ourselves lovingly.

Metatron greatly assists those labeled with ADD/ADHD as well as those labeled with being bipolar or manic depressive. This touches on just one of his areas of specialty: balance. Those labeled with ADD, ADHD, or bipolar disorder can be overwhelmed with life due to their sensitivities. They are extremely sensitive souls, and therefore, can have severe reactions to food, noise, color, texture, and energy. They can also be labeled as empathic; feeling the sadness, joy, and instability from all. Yes, from *all*. This type of gift can be overwhelming, and many find themselves taking drugs, prescription or other-wise, to deaden the pain they feel. These beautiful souls can feel energetically unsafe as society continues to tell them to fit in, stop being so sensitive, and grow up. Chatting more with Metatron will lead to ways to soften the harsh-ness and ultimately empower them and you.

Metatron also assists with writing. This holds true particularly if the writing is channeled information. He deciphers information, helping to make it understandable while holding the vibration of it at its highest level. This includes offering insights to symbols, geometric shapes, and all things sacred.

Zodiac Association

Metatron connects with the astrological sign of Virgo. Virgos are well known perfectionists, and having known many in my life, I tend to agree! While per-fectionism isn't a natural human trait, it's why Metatron is there to assist. He gently reminds us that we are perfectly imperfect. Anything man-made can be improved upon. Therefore, don't wait until it is perfect or you'll drive yourself nuts in the attempt, which would be a shame, because you have much to offer!

Metatron's Name Defined

Metatron's name is translated to mean "one who occupies the throne next to the throne of the divine." In other words, Metatron sits to one side of God. He knows all, your deepest fears as well as desires. He may point out your fears only to motive you to snap out of it, while presenting you with ideas and opportunities to keep you on track with your soul's mission. It's one of the reasons I've dubbed Metatron the Motivator. He greatly helps keep you on track, focused, and motivated in what you are here to do.

Angelic Encounter

Speaking of motivation . . . Metatron has "wing-slapped" me more times than I care to admit. He has snapped me out of a funk when I *think* events aren't moving as quickly as they should. This book is a prime example. It's taken years, truly years, to get it to this space. I wrote like a fiend, thinking it was the next best thing to Shakespeare, until reality checked in and it was shelved. Over time, customers and clients alike began asking me to train them and to write a book on angels (these kinds of events are the gentlest kind of wing-slap), so off the shelf it came, until life's shiny moments would happen and it would be shelved once more.

And so on.

Just when I thought it wasn't meant to be, clients began harassing (yes, harassing me!) to finish it and teach them.

I sat with Metatron deep in meditation one day. He entered, chuckling, shaking his head; he even clucked at me! All the while I never felt less than, stupid, or unworthy.

"Little one, *now* is the time to finish this project. Now is the time. You and the world are ready. Now is the time to compile this work and present it back to the world so they will remember."

Okay, Metatron, this will be no small feat, but *yes!*

You hold in your hand the result.

Metatron's Light Temple

Metatron's light temple is in Luxor, Egypt. If you think about it, this shouldn't be surprising since Egypt is often thought of as an ancient civilization; pyramids, pharaohs, and more. Metatron is just this; full of ancient information about geometry and how geometry is gently infused into our daily living; whether or not you excelled in math at school, geometry is part of your day-to-day life!

Metatron's Symbol

Envision yourself as the dot from the symbol. Your energy shoots out, grabs information, and brings it down so it can assimilate within your body. It does not just assimilate, but also absorbs into your psyche, giving you greater insight into who you are and what you are here to do. It then shoots up even higher, bringing it down, and so on. This "and so on" phase never ends, for you are constantly evolving and stepping more into your greatness. With each step you expand ever higher, so you can soar in all areas of your life. Each step launches you more into your brilliance and presents another step to chat with Uriel, allowing you to feel safe to be you.

Life is but one adventure of self-growth after another, and Metatron's symbol signifies this, as each adventure experienced is another opportunity for spiritual growth.

Metatron's Compass Direction

Metatron has no known compass directions. He oversees all and therefore incorporates all directions. He is just cool like that.

Metatron's Chakra Association

Metatron oversees the soul star chakra. The soul star represents this ever-expansive energy encompassing all colors in the color spectrum, taking all under his direction of spiritual evolution and ascension. This chakra is located approximately six inches above your head. The soul star chakra is also known

as the gateway to the soul, the energy center of your higher self. It is frequently called the gateway, since it is situated outside the physical body,
allowing deeper information to flow through you. The soul star chakra does
not regulate any one specific area of your body, but helps the entire body on
all levels: physical, mental, emotional, and spiritual. At this specific chakra,
you are a spark of source energy. If indeed you are a spark of that source, you
are then complete and encapsulate all elements: earth, water, fire, metal, and
air; another reason why Metatron does not only have one compass direction.

Think of your soul star and earth star chakra as twins, just like Metatron
and Sandalphon. Both balance out the other; the yin and yang of chakras.
You can reach for the heavens while being fully present and grounded in this
dimension.

As Above, So Below.

The Alpha and the Omega.

Male and Female.

Light and Dark.

Together, they create the perfect balance and enable you to manifest a
life that is perfect for you. As they are ever present in your life, they would
naturally join together in the middle: your heart. Allowing you to be ever
expansive, grounded, and living from your center. Living from the true source
of love.

The soul star chakra keeps you aligned and helps you stay true to your
soul's mission by keeping a distance from the human/ego-driven dramas surrounding you. Remember, when you stay true to self, events can quickly line
up to keep you on track. But if you are battling against the rapids or seem to
be consistently banging your head against the proverbial wall, your soul star
chakra may be out of alignment. Quietly go to your heart and reconnect with
your soul and allow the angels to step in to gently guide you.

Angelic Activity

As you most likely have picked up by now, Metatron is associated with sacred geometry. This kind of geometry is evident throughout nature: the beehive, the inside of a conch shell, the beautiful symmetry of a flower. It's all about balance. Geometry, you may recall from your high school days, encompasses many shapes: squares, circles, triangles, tetrahedrons, pentagrams, and more. This is Metatron's area of expertise; noticing and embracing those subtle nuances connecting to shapes throughout your day that help create a more observant, present, and dynamic you.

Therefore, depending where you are on your spiritual journey, here is Metatron's activity: begin in nature. Be observant. Notice the symmetry of a tree leaf, a flower, or any animal. It is beyond perfect. Balance exists in this perfection. As your horizons begin to expand within nature, take it beyond. Begin to play with it; how many squares or circles or triangles do you see throughout your day, whether man-made or found in nature?

Want to go more urban and look at man-made items? Here's a great place to start: a bridge! No fooling. Notice how many triangles are incorporated in every bridge you cross. Once you start, it's difficult to stop, but oh, so much fun!

Each step is another way to share how much the angels are indeed always with you and show the many ways in which they present themselves to you.

Metatron's Healing Crystals

The diamond and clear quartz are Metatron's signature crystals. Both encompass the entire color spectrum as we know it. Think about it, haven't you ever been dazzled by a diamond or clear quartz as they catch the light? You see all sorts of colors: blues, yellows, purples, greens, and much more. These crystals represent the spark of the divine within you, allowing you to shine your truest essence so all may appreciate your inner as well as outer beauty.

Clear quartz is known as the master crystal because it encompasses all the colors of the spectrum. Just as Metatron has no one specific compass direction, clear quartz has no one area of expertise. Clear quartz is one of the few crystals that can truly be programmed to help you in certain areas of your life.

Programmed? True! Because clear quartz holds all energy, you can actually work with it for a very specific purpose. If you wish to explore and improve a specific area of your life, obtaining a clear quartz and then sitting with it in meditation with your intent in mind can help illuminate the variety of ways to help you achieve your goals. Keep in mind, as with angels, crystals will not adhere to assisting you in any devious or unsavory undertaking. Clear quartz is incredibly easy to find, from your science museum shops, metaphysical stores, and quite often in nature itself!

Angelic Aromatherapy

Some of my favorite scents that connect with Metatron are:

Chamomile: for opening higher chakras which can offer deeper dream states.
Sandalwood: used for spiritual awareness while dispelling negative energy. Also works as a great balancing energy, as it is one of Sandalphon's key scents.
Frankincense: offers strong vibrations. An excellent choice for meditation incenses and mixtures used to promote spiritual growth and induce visions.
Grapefruit: assists with mental clarity, self-confidence, overcoming self-doubt, insecurities, and negative emotions that keep one bonded to the pain of past experiences, to help deal with jealousy, envy, despondency, bitterness, and releasing frustration.

In closing, I wish to share these words of wisdom:

Before your soul descended to this world, it was determined it would succeed. If not in this lifetime, then in another, or yet another—eventually it will fulfill the entire mission.

And in each lifetime, it will move further ahead.
It was this knowledge that conceived it.
It was this inspiration that brought the world to be.

It is this vision of success,
That lies at the essence of all things.

Metatron's Askfirmations

Why is it so easy for me to connect with and understand spiritual messages?
Why is it so easy for me to understand sacred geometry?
Why is it so easy for me to embrace my spiritual path?

Metatron's Fun Fact

Metatron and Michael both oversee the spiritual evolution of all, but specifically those labeled as indigo, crystal, and rainbow.

Guided Meditation with Archangel Metatron

Sit facing any specific direction that is comfortable for you.

Breathe in for four counts,
Hold for four counts,
Breathe out for four counts.

Call on Archangel Michael and his legions,
To stand guard while you meditate.

Breathe in for four counts,
Hold for four counts,
Breathe out for four counts.

The room fills.
It gets warmer,
As Michael and his legion enter to stand guard,
During this meditation.

Breathe in for four counts,
Hold for four counts,
Breathe out for four counts.

It is now time to call on,
Archangel Metatron.

Breathe in for four counts,
Hold for four counts,
Breathe out for four counts.

As Metatron enters,
The room becomes brighter.

Breathe in for four counts,
Hold for four counts,
Breathe out for four counts.

With each breath,
The brilliance increases.

Breathe in for four counts,
Hold for four counts,
Breathe out for four counts.

Metatron's presence becomes stronger,
More alive,
More real.

Breathe in for four counts,
Hold for four counts,
Breathe out for four counts.

As he comes even closer,
A thought comes to mind.
"How can I help you, little one?"

Breathe in for four counts,
Hold for four counts,
Breathe out for four counts.

You know you are being listened to.
You know you are being heard.
You know you may share,
Anything with him.

Breathe in for four counts,
Hold for four counts,
Breathe out for four counts.

And you share.

Breathe in for four counts,
Hold for four counts,
Breathe out for four counts.

You share your woes,
You share your dreams,
You share your heaviness.

Breathe in for four counts,
Hold for four counts,
Breathe out for four counts.

With each breath,
Metatron eases a bit of your angst.

Breathe in for four counts,
Hold for four counts,
Breathe out for four counts.

With each breath,
Metatron implants a new thought,
A new idea,
A new way to interpret.

Breathe in for four counts,
Hold for four counts,
Breathe out for four counts.

With each breath,
Metatron shares with you,
Visions of your future.

Breathe in for four counts,
Hold for four counts,
Breathe out for four counts.

The future of how you are meant to live,
The future of the love,
The support,
The joy,
The health,
That surrounds you.

Breathe in for four counts,
Hold for four counts,
Breathe out for four counts.

With each breath,
Your heart becomes a bit lighter,
Fuller,
Much like puzzle pieces sliding together.

Breathe in for four counts,
Hold for four counts,
Breathe out for four counts.

Keep breathing,
And allow the brilliance to fill your soul.

Breathe in for four counts,
Hold for four counts,
Breathe out for four counts.

Repeat.

Breathe in for four counts,
Hold for four counts,
Breathe out for four counts.

Know that you may enter this sacred union,
Upon a moment's notice.

Breathe in for four counts,
Hold for four counts,
Breathe out for four counts.

Metatron softly reminds you that he will always be there for you.

Breathe in for four counts,
Hold for four counts,
Breathe out for four counts.

He reminds you that he walks behind you,
In front of you,
And beside you,
Gently guiding your path.

Breathe in for four counts,
Hold for four counts,
Breathe out for four counts.

Repeat.

Breathe in for four counts,
Hold for four counts,
Breathe out for four counts.

As this meditation comes to an end,
You feel the presence of a hand on top of your head,
As in a blessing.

Breathe in for four counts,
Hold for four counts,
Breathe out for four counts.

That is exactly what has just transpired.
A blessing has been placed upon you.

Breathe in for four counts,
Hold for four counts,
Breathe out for four counts.

As you continue to soak in the energy,
The room begins to be more present.

Breathe in for four counts,
Hold for four counts,
Breathe out for four counts.

As Metatron prepares to depart for the time being,
The room and its noises,
Begin to ground you.

Breathe in for four counts,
Hold for four counts,
Breathe out for four counts.

You feel your body once more.

Breathe in for four counts,
Hold for four counts,
Breathe out for four counts.

You wiggle your toes and hands.

Breathe in for four counts,
Hold for four counts,
Breathe out for four counts.

You slowly open your eyes.

Breathe in for four counts,
Hold for four counts,
Breathe out for four counts.

You inhale deeply and exhale loudly.
Welcome back.

12

Archangel Auriel

Angel of Illumination

"Allow me to assist you by illuminating the next steps that are best for you on the path called life."

—Archangel Auriel

Auriel is often confused with Uriel. Easy to understand, given the name similarities. Let's put this to rest immediately—they are different! Just as two people who may be named Johnny and Jon; similar, but extremely different. However, Auriel's connection to Uriel is more than similar; she is known to be the feminine aspect of Uriel in the ongoing theme of balance. As Uriel is about safety, Auriel assists with illumination and seeing the truth. When you combine their energies, Uriel helps you feel safe to be you, while Auriel illuminates the proper path for you.

Zodiac Association

Auriel shares the zodiac sign of Cancer with Gabriel. Why? Simply because the moon is Cancer's ruling planet. Since Auriel is the lunar angel, no further explanation is necessary! Like Gabriel, Auriel honors your energy. Do you need to be quieter during a new moon? Then do so. Is it time to shout from the rooftops who you are during a full moon? Howl away! The moon is long-known to draw out high energy. Babies are born during a full moon. More crimes are committed during a full moon. Bottom line: pull in your shell when needed and come out and share when warranted.

Auriel's Name Defined

Auriel's name means "light of God." Think of a beautiful full moon night. It can illuminate the world in a soft glow, adding mysticism to your surroundings, while adding clarity to burning questions. Auriel is often called the angel of destiny. She helps illuminate your chosen path, enabling you to walk more confidently. Auriel's energy is very soothing and calming, yet there is great power underneath it all. Remember, power is power; it is up to you to decide how that power is shared and executed. Will you choose soft or harsh? Love or hate? Joy or sorrow? You always have a choice.

Angelic Encounter

Like the rest of my angelic gang members, I chat with Auriel on a regular basis, especially on those beautiful full moon nights when I can't sleep. We have had many a chat over tea in the middle of the night. Good thing my husband sleeps soundly!

Certainly, the most memorable of these conversations concerned not only the unveiling of this book, but Auriel clarifying in great detail my gifts and mission in this life. While the conversation lasted a solid hour, it is something that I still hold private. What I will share is this: continue to read, get connected with me through various social media outlets, and you will witness firsthand who I am and why I am here.

Auriel's Light Temple

As you read more of Auriel in this chapter, you will quickly understand the location of Auriel's light temple: the moon. The moon's energy is known to affect the sea, causing higher tides than normal, especially during a storm surge. More babies are born during a full moon, and unfortunately, the likelihood of crime also increases during the full moon's energy. Ever hear of the term *lunatic*? It directly comes from this lunar angel and is a nod to the power of the moon. I'm no different; I spend many sleepless nights during a full moon, as do quite a few of my clients. If this resonates with you, I suggest you keep a moon journal to note how your personal energy fares every day, and then note what cycle the moon is in to help you move to the next step in your empowerment journey. Once you better understand how the various cycles of the moon affect you, you will know ahead of time what days you tend to be more energized or the days you wish to spend more quality time alone.

Auriel's Symbol

Auriel's symbol demonstrates how information is slowly infused into your energetic field, and then shot out for more. Start at the symbol's dot and move straight up. This is you standing taller and more confidently. As you do this, you are reaching into the universe, grabbing the information, and letting it filter into your very being. That is the key word: filter. It softly fills your being with light. Softly fills your being with information. Softly fills you with better clarity on your next step(s). When it is delivered in this manner, the effect is longer lasting. As you get more comfortable with this newfangled form of communication, it will be delivered quicker and with greater ease.

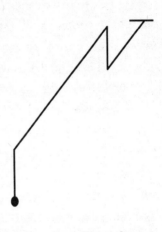

Auriel's Compass Direction

I chatted with Auriel regarding her compass direction. This is what she shared: "While I do not resonate with a specific compass direction, I suggest that people connect me with due north. Why is this? Because, as you know, all compasses align with the direction of north, just as humans ultimately desire to find their true north. This is how I assist them; to find their true north and align them with their soul mission."

Well, there ya go!

True north, it is.

Auriel's Chakra Association

Uriel oversees the root chakra, while Auriel oversees the angelic chakra, also known as the fifth eye chakra. This one is rather difficult to locate, but is approximately six inches above your soul star chakra and toward the back. To offer a better visual, imagine your skull and locate the back corner. Go up diagonally about twelve inches. This is the approximate location of the angelic chakra. In fact, if you look at Auriel's symbol, it reflects this chakra's position.

The angelic chakra's name hints at its area of expertise, as it helps strengthen your true angelic self while strengthening the connection with the angelic kingdom. Angelic self? Yes, all have an angelic side to them. Does this mean all are incarnated angels? Hardly, but we all have a spiritual side, angelic if you will, that guides us when we listen to the whisperings of our soul.

If this chakra is out of balance, you may experience restlessness, over-worrying, and general disharmony with life. When the angelic chakra is in balance, the chatter is nonstop from the angelic realm. You recognize them for who they are and how they are ever present in your life and gladly welcome them to join in. Does this mean you literally hear voices? No. Remember, we discussed the various clairs in Raziel's chapter (p. 126). What this means is that you more easily discern the angelic chatter from the ego chatter. You are able to more easily receive messages from the angels and, if needed, to pass onto friends, family, strangers, and clients.

Angelic Activity

The energy of the full moon, as mentioned earlier, is quite powerful. Why not harness that energy in a more personal and productive way?

Look at the chart below.

Moon Phase	Significance
New	New beginnings, fresh start, blank slate
Waxing Crescent	Intention, hopes, wishes
First Quarter	Challenges, decisions, action
Waxing Gibbous	Adjust, refine, edit
Full	Signed, sealed, stamped
Waning Gibbous	Gratitude, sharing, enthusiasm
Last Quarter	Release, let go, forgive
Waning Crescent	Surrender, rest, recuperate

Pick just one phase and its correlating energy. Decide which area you would like to explore more within your personal life. During the next phase of the moon's cycle, consciously delve deeper into the whys in your life and see what answers become illuminated for you. Don't judge the inspirational thoughts you may get! Each one is given to help empower you. If it feels too difficult, explore the reasoning behind that, as well. Keep chatting with Auriel, and she will help illuminate all the right answers for you. Her only question is "Will you listen with open ears and heart?"

Auriel's Healing Crystal

Moonstone is Auriel's crystal choice. These similarities are sublime. Moonstone, as Auriel, offers tranquil, soothing energies that can offer deeper insight into emotional patterns and dream interpretation. Who hasn't had a dream that, upon awakening, you wished there was an interpreter nearby? Other great energetic properties of moonstone can include an amulet of protection for travelers and a path to wisdom. Moonstone is known to calm and encourage, presenting the idea of going with the natural rhythms of life.

As there are many phases of the moon, there are many variations of moonstone. For example, gray moonstone is more associated with new moon energies; it assists one seeing beyond the veil and perceiving information that has been hidden with greater clarity. White is, you guessed it, full moon energies and can help translate and decipher dreams. Peach and/or yellow moonstone softens the energies surrounding the heart to help sooth anxiety. Investigate your desires and better yet, when purchasing a moonstone, see which one speaks most to you and then look up its particular meaning and mission. You may get more than you bargained for in a very good way!

Angelic Aromatherapy

Auriel, like all the angels, has magical scents that are associated with her. Here are some of my favorites:

Cypress: it is known to relieve anxiety. Think about it, if you are anxious, it is certainly much harder to find your true path.

Neroli: for its own properties of decreasing blood pressure, which can be connected to anxiety and stress.

Benzoin of Sumatra: it is known to uplift one's spirit and outlook on life. When these three scents are combined, you get a less stressed, more joyful energy; a rather grand combination!

Auriel's Askfirmations

Why is it so easy for me to understand the moon cycles?

Why is it so easy for me to interpret my dreams?

Why is it so easy for me to relax and use softer energies?

Why is it so easy for me to embrace my destiny?

Auriel's Fun Fact

The hummingbird is the animal associated with Auriel. Her plant? The moonflower.

Guided Meditation with Archangel Auriel

Sit in any direction that is comfortable for you.

If looking for a clearer direction on any path, please face north.

Breathe in for four counts,

Hold for four counts,

Breathe out for four counts.

Call on Archangel Michael and his legions,

To stand guard while you meditate.

Breathe in for four counts,

Hold for four counts,

Breathe out for four counts.

The room fills.
It gets warmer,
As Michael and his legion enter to stand guard,
During this meditation.

Breathe in for four counts,
Hold for four counts,
Breathe out for four counts.

It is now time to call on,
Archangel Auriel.

The room begins to pulsate and glow.

Breathe in for four counts,
Hold for four counts,
Breathe out for four counts.

Auriel brings with her a lantern that casts its glow,
In the exact phase the moon is in today.

Breathe in for four counts,
Hold for four counts,
Breathe out for four counts.

As Auriel continues to step forward,
She lays before you a road not yet traveled by you.

Breathe in for four counts,
Hold for four counts,
Breathe out for four counts.

She shines her lantern on the road,
And you begin to see glimpses of what is to be in your future.

Breathe in for four counts,
Hold for four counts,
Breathe out for four counts.

Repeat.

Breathe in for four counts,
Hold for four counts,
Breathe out for four counts.

On this road, you see before you a flight of steps.

Breathe in for four counts,
Hold for four counts,
Breathe out for four counts.

As you approach the steps,
They widen and allow you to scale them with great ease.

Breathe in for four counts,
Hold for four counts,
Breathe out for four counts.

As you climb the steps,
Adorning the walls are portraits of people;
Some you recognize, some are new to you.

Breathe in for four counts,
Hold for four counts,
Breathe out for four counts.

These people are and will be in your life to help you grow,
And reach your goals.

Breathe in for four counts,
Hold for four counts,
Breathe out for four counts.

You reach the top of the steps and see before you a road that is littered,
With rocks, pebbles, and boulders.

Breathe in for four counts,
Hold for four counts,
Breathe out for four counts.

You feel somewhat dismayed.
Look at all those detours and road blocks!

Breathe in for four counts,
Hold for four counts,
Breathe out for four counts.

Fear not, dearest soul,
Allow me to vaporize each one,
So your path is clear.
Remember, each detour and block is man-made,
And can easily be removed with a bit of faith in yourself.

Breathe in for four counts,
Hold for four counts,
Breathe out for four counts.

Repeat.

Breathe in for four counts,
Hold for four counts,
Breathe out for four counts.

As Auriel casts the light from her lantern onto each block,
You feel a load lightening from within.

Breathe in for four counts,
Hold for four counts,
Breathe out for four counts.

Repeat.

Breathe in for four counts,
Hold for four counts,
Breathe out for four counts.

Stay on this road for as long as you desire.

Breathe in for four counts,
Hold for four counts,
Breathe out for four counts.

Feel the load lighten,
Feel your soul becoming lighter,
Feel the energy flowing through your being with greater love.

Breathe in for four counts,
Hold for four counts,
Breathe out for four counts.

Today's adventure is about to come to a close,
But Auriel reminds you that this is just the beginning,
Of embracing you and your mission with greater passion.

Breathe in for four counts,
Hold for four counts,
Breathe out for four counts.

You feel your body once more.

Breathe in for four counts,
Hold for four counts,
Breathe out for four counts.

You wiggle your toes and hands.

Breathe in for four counts,
Hold for four counts,
Breathe out for four counts.

You slowly open your eyes.

Breathe in for four counts,
Hold for four counts,
Breathe out for four counts.

You inhale deeply and exhale loudly.
Welcome back.

13

Archangel Shamael

Angel of Harmony

"Life can be harmonious or tumultuous. Which do you choose?"

—Archangel Shamael

Shamael is known as the angel of harmony, as well as the angel of sacred sound. Sacred sound includes mantras, chants, instrumental music, songs, as well as the human voice. Doesn't your heart melt when another expresses their love for you? Isn't it a sacred feeling being publicly recognized for your gifts, no matter what they may be? It's all sacred.

Music has been known to soothe the soul, excite the senses, and transport one to another place and time. Have you ever heard a song from your past only to be transported to that moment? Just as similarly, holiday songs harken to a simpler time of love, community, and magic. Jazz can get one going. Meditation music can assist in quieting the senses, allowing one to expand their aura and field. Each musical genre offers a gift of expression and expansion, not only for the musicians, but for the listeners.

All songs can do this. If a song is played from your childhood, teenage years, first real date, and other important moments of your life, the door opens and the memories come forth. Equally powerful, music can hint at a past life. For example, I really enjoy music from the twenties. I am certainly not old enough to remember it firsthand in this life, but could it be from another? I also hold a great fondness for slave songs. While it does harken to a more than troubled time, I find the songs soothing. This is what music can do for you: it opens the heart, the imagination, and memories. If you are curious about past lives, think of the older music that calls to you. Have you ever wondered why? How does it affect you? If this is something that speaks to you, investigate a certified past life regressionist and don't forget to call on Michael prior to your session!

You can create your own music by playing with a crystal bowl. These bowls have been crafted to sing at a certain pitch and are highly effective for healing, meditation, and soul openings. I have many tools to tone with. I wouldn't part with my angel aura bowl, as it truly transports me to a different place. I am also quite fond of song pods, a Native American tool used in healing. They are typically a type of metal on the outside and are filled with crystals and other good medicine at the heart. They've been proven to expand your aura while smoothing it. I use these as a finishing touch when seeing clients for healing sessions.

Water is a conductor (no pun intended—no, really, no pun intended!) of energy. It's why many folks love being by the ocean and/or a lake. It not only soothes the soul, but can offer keen insights in a very non obtrusive way that allows one to be accepting. It can excite (think surfing). It can provide new paths upon which to tread. Water does this and much more. If you have ever vacationed by the beach, you understand this. There are times when just sitting and listening to the surf can be relaxing and rejuvenating. It's during those moments of connection to the water that answers can filter in. Ideas can become clearer. In fact, in the course of writing this book, there were many days I could do no more. I took a break, frolicked in the ocean or snow and came back refreshed (yes, it took that long to write!).

Some people are so affected by water, they get plenty of messages while taking a shower—to the point they call it showerology! Try it yourself. When pondering a situation, ask a question prior to your bath or shower. Let it go and see what insight you receive while bathing.

Water can assist in the release of toxins from the body. This is why after any energy treatment—acupuncture, Reiki or other healing modality, massage, yoga, etc.—it is imperative to drink as much pure water as possible. It is through those modalities and any aerobic activity that the body works harder to rid itself of things that are not serving it well. Water helps tremendously to flush the bad out. Chatting with Shamael will offer insight into how many glasses a day is appropriate for you, as there is no right amount. Each person is different, and therefore requires a different amount of water to keep not only their body lubricated and running smoothly, but to prevent toxins from taking up residency.

Zodiac Association

Shamael is all about the water and the flow. Therefore, it probably doesn't come as a surprise that Shamael connects with the zodiac sign of Pisces. While Pisceans tend to be very intuitive, their biggest hurdle is learning to go with the flow. To take on the essence of a duck and let things roll off more easily. To not get caught up in the minutiae of life. Why? Because of their strong intuitive connection, many Pisceans literally take on the weight of the world of those around them, which can leave them feeling depressed. Not a great way to live life! Chat with Shamael to learn how to be like a duck.

Shamael's Name Defined

Shamael's name can be loosely translated as "the divining herald" and/or "the angel of song." Which makes total sense since Shamael is the angel of harmony. He heralds in to announce you have arrived at a more profound and illuminated sense of self. In other words, it is time to toot your horn!

Angelic Encounter

Here's a story to hopefully bring home the message: I was writing my first children's book and having issues with one passage. The angels said get to the beach. Of course, I argued. I wanted to finish the book, who had time for such frivolity as going to the beach? This, ahem, discussion continued for well over forty-five minutes. Ultimately, they won (never argue with them, you really never win). The entire fifteen minutes it took to get to the beach, I grumbled. Complained, even. I *needed* to finish the passage! Grumbled, grumbled, grumbled. Seriously, who argues about going to the beach? Grumbled some more and unpacked the car, set up my chair, etc. Still grumbling, I got into the water. Within moments, I kid you not, I had the passage! I raced out of the water with people staring at me, probably thinking what is this mad woman going on about? I finally sat down to write it, and it made the final cut of the book.

Shamael's Light Temple

Shamael's temple is in Antarctica, and with all the frozen water and snow in that area, is it any wonder he is also associated with water? Within each snowflake or frozen molecule of water, energy is stored. One can only imagine the information that is stored deep within!

Shamael's Symbol

Look at Shamael's symbol. It is reminiscent of a clef used when writing music, is it not? Life may throw that periodic curve ball, but that is no reason to follow its drama queue and play along. Use of Shamael's symbol is sure to bring a lightness to your world, while introducing the concept of adagio; ease, peace, and harmony.

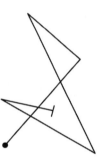

Shamael's Compass Direction

Shamael's compass direction is associated with the south. It will be an easy one to remember, as his name begins with *S* and his light temple is Antarctica, about as far south as one can get! As Shamael's messages tie so closely with water and harmony and, as mentioned, ancient knowledge is literally frozen in the icebergs and landscape of Antarctica, it ought to come as no surprise that south is his direction of choice.

Shamael's Chakra Association

Like other angels before him, such as Metatron, Shamael has no known chakra association. As you listen to music, does it not affect all of your chakras, sometimes all at once? As you drink water, are you not giving to all of you at one time?

Think about it: music uplifts the soul to help you ground and soar (earth star and soul star chakras). Belting out a song no matter your locale can be scary or empowering (root and solar plexus). Writing lyrics for a song is highly creative (sacral), hearing or singing a song can bring on those happy tears (heart), and music can be transcendental (third eye and crown). All it takes is a bit of imagination to see how the entire body can be and is affected by music.

While not chakra connected, Shamael's colors are a combination of indigo, violet, and gold, creating a resplendent vision indeed. It creates a symphony of colors that melds into a beautiful serenade.

Angel Activity

Dr. Masaru Emoto is the forerunning scientist concerning water and the energy it holds. One of his more popular books is *The Hidden Messages in Water*. This book demonstrates how water molecules shift depending on the thoughts that are directed at it. If you think fear as you hold your cup of tea, you end up drinking fear. If you feel expansion and abundance while holding your glass of water, you drink expansion and abundance. And so on.

Why does this happen? The high water content in all living things conducts sound (keeping in mind that words are sound) to heal at a deep molecular level. This can even go so deep as to affect and help heal at a soul level. Think of patients who have been in a coma. Upon awakening, many of them report that they knew who was with them by what they *heard*.

There have been studies done in elementary schools with this philosophy in mind. Two jars were filled with rice. One word, such as love or hate, was taped on the outside of each jar. Students would walk by and simply say that word. The love jar looked pristine after one week while the hate jar was moldy and completely decomposing. Experiment yourself. Within a week, the results just may amaze you. Just more proof that words do indeed have power.

Here's what you can do now: infuse all your beverages with the great energies of positivity; love, abundance, healing, joy, and more. Notice over time, how the taste of the beverage now actually tastes better! Why wouldn't it, you are truly now "intaking" a life force!

You could even help the universe the next time you are near a lake, pond, ocean, river, etc. by simply saying positive words, such as healing, pure, or love. These words can help change the water over time. How? One can only imagine, but perhaps the water will become noticed more and all will wish to help keep it cleaner.

Shamael's Healing Crystal

Shamael's crystal of choice is aquamarine, the birthstone of March. Energetically, it is well known for past life recall and all work related to that. Aquamarine is known to assist with calming communication issues. It should come as no surprise that it is associated with the sea and can protect travelers on water, such as sailors, fishermen, etc. It can help reduce fluid retention. Lastly, it is a great meditation tool to bring about a sense of peace and harmony. If this doesn't have Shamael's energy, what stone would?

Angelic Aromatherapy

Patchouli is one of my favorite scents associated with Shamael, for it helps to awaken the senses and allow one's self to go with the flow of life. Another is frankincense. **Frankincense** is a very sacred oil, and as Shamael assists with sacred sound, it connects the two quite profoundly. Lastly, is myrrh. **Myrrh** is often used to anoint another or an object. Isn't it time you anointed yourself with the recognition that you are a divine soul?

Shamael's Askfirmations

Why is it so easy for me to drink plenty of water?
Why is it so easy for me to hear the perfect music for this situation?
Why is it so easy for me to allow the messages of the angels to come through?

Shamael's Fun Facts

★ Shamael is often touted as an aspect of Metatron, and I would have to agree! As Metatron is your soul's mission instigator, Shamael helps to make it easier in a more harmonious way.

★ Shamael was instrumental in the creation of all. As water is life, this also makes a lovely connection back to his area of expertise!

Guided Meditation with Archangel Shamael

Sit facing any direction.

Breathe in for four counts,
Hold for four counts,
Breathe out for four counts.

Call on Archangel Michael and his legions,
To stand guard while you meditate.

Breathe in for four counts,
Hold for four counts,
Breathe out for four counts.

The room fills.
It gets warmer,
As Michael and his legions enter to stand guard,
During this meditation.

Breathe in for four counts,
Hold for four counts,
Breathe out for four counts.

It is now time to call on,
Shamael.

The room begins to pulsate and glow.

Breathe in for four counts,
Hold for four counts,
Breathe out for four counts.

Shamael makes his entrance,
Followed by a band playing your favorite upbeat music.

Breathe in for four counts,
Hold for four counts,
Breathe out for four counts.

As you enjoy your private concert,
Shamael, the orchestra leader, steps forward.

Breathe in for four counts,
Hold for four counts,
Breathe out for four counts.

The band continues to serenade you.

Breathe in for four counts,
Hold for four counts,
Breathe out for four counts.

As Shamael comes closer,
He reaches out a hand and asks you to dance.

Breathe in for four counts,
Hold for four counts,
Breathe out for four counts.

As you clasp Shamael's hand,
You are brought to your feet,
And you begin to sway and dance in perfect harmony.

Breathe in for four counts,
Hold for four counts,
Breathe out for four counts.

As you twirl around the room,
Shamael reminds you that life is but a harmonious ride.

Breathe in for four counts,
Hold for four counts,
Breathe out for four counts.

As any song goes,
There are verses and choruses.
What is your chorus,
That you find yourself repeating,
Throughout life?

Breathe in for four counts,
Hold for four counts,
Breathe out for four counts.

Repeat.

Breathe in for four counts,
Hold for four counts,
Breathe out for four counts.

What does your chorus tell yourself?
What comes to mind?
Shamael asks,
"Does your chorus serve you well?"

Breathe in for four counts,
Hold for four counts,
Breathe out for four counts.

If it does not,
How would you change it?

Breathe in for four counts,
Hold for four counts,
Breathe out for four counts.

What will you now begin to sing?

Breathe in for four counts,
Hold for four counts,
Breathe out for four counts.

How will you begin to dance through life?

Breathe in for four counts,
Hold for four counts,
Breathe out for four counts.

Ask for guidance from Shamael, the angel of harmony,
If you wish to switch your chorus.

Breathe in for four counts,
Hold for four counts,
Breathe out for four counts.

Shamael will only be too glad to assist in giving you a new one.

Breathe in for four counts,
Hold for four counts,
Breathe out for four counts.

Listen softly as the music plays your chorus.

Breathe in for four counts,
Hold for four counts,
Breathe out for four counts.

Repeat.

Breathe in for four counts,
Hold for four counts,
Breathe out for four counts.

Your chorus expands your heart chakra.

Breathe in for four counts,
Hold for four counts,
Breathe out for four counts.

Your chorus makes you smile.

Breathe in for four counts,
Hold for four counts,
Breathe out for four counts.

Your chorus brings happy angel tears to your eyes.

Breathe in for four counts,
Hold for four counts,
Breathe out for four counts.

Of course, it does, it is yours!

Breathe in for four counts,
Hold for four counts,
Breathe out for four counts.

Dance with your chorus.

Breathe in for four counts,
Hold for four counts,
Breathe out for four counts.

Sing out your chorus.

Breathe in for four counts,
Hold for four counts,
Breathe out for four counts.

Drink in your chorus.

Breathe in for four counts,
Hold for four counts,
Breathe out for four counts.

Feel it pulsate your soul,
And excite your being.

Breathe in for four counts,
Hold for four counts,
Breathe out for four counts.

Embrace it,
Own it,
Live it.

Breathe in for four counts,
Hold for four counts,
Breathe out for four counts.

As the dancing begins to slow,
Your chorus continues to play,
But much softer.

Breathe in for four counts,
Hold for four counts,
Exhale for four counts.

Shamael reminds you that this is your song.
It can uplift you at a moment's notice.

Breathe in for four counts,
Hold for four counts,
Exhale for four counts.

Today's meditation is coming to an end,
But you are reminded, as always,
All you need do is ask, and all the angels are with you.

Breathe in for four counts,
Hold for four counts,
Breathe out for four counts.

You feel your body once more.

Breathe in for four counts,
Hold for four counts,
Breathe out for four counts.

You wiggle your toes and hands.

Breathe in for four counts,
Hold for four counts,
Breathe out for four counts.

You inhale deeply and exhale loudly.
Welcome back.

14

Archangel Thuriel

Angel of Animals

"To understand an animal's message, one must quiet the mind and listen with the heart."

—Archangel Thuriel

Thuriel is not as well known as, say, Big Mike, but it doesn't make him any less significant in your world, especially if you have a pet, are a pet sitter, veterinary technician, veterinary doctor, groomer, zoologist, animal trainer, etc. If you are in any of these fields, chat with Thuriel to become more insightful regarding your charges and better understand the inner knowings of what is going on with the animal before you.

Just as each angel has other angels in their legion that assist with the same purpose, there are many angels working with Thuriel that support specific animal kingdoms. Angels such as (listed alphabetically):

★ **Arael:** angel of aviary. Arael oversees both wild and domesticated birds.
★ **Behemiel:** angel of "tame" animals. This is for those animals that are trained to perform.
★ **Desmorael:** angel of extinct animals. This includes animals that fall under the mythical category such as unicorns, Pegasus, etc.
★ **Feskael:** angel of canines. Feskael oversees both wild and domesticated dogs.

- ★ **Hariel:** angel of "fur babies." Think of your beloved pets.
- ★ **Josphirael:** angel of insecta. Even those "lowly" insects deserve angelic assistance!
- ★ **Manakel:** angel of aquatic animals. Wild and domesticated fish, and other sea creatures.
- ★ **Mesmeriael:** angel of aquatic mammals. Mesmeriael oversees the wild and tame sea mammal. Tame? Think SeaWorld and other zoos that not only hold these animals but have trained them to perform.
- ★ **Miquiriel:** angel of equines. Miquiriel oversees the wild and domesticated horse.
- ★ **Respirael:** angel of reptiles. Perfect for snakes, lizards, chameleons, etc.
- ★ **Sesmoreal:** angel of felines. Sesmoreal oversees the wild and domesticated cats.

You may have noticed three different categories: wild, tame, and domesticated. Wild is just that. The animal enjoys life in their natural habitat unencumbered by rules and are left to their own devices. As such, they are unpredictable in their actions but live life as it was meant to be for them.

There are many animals that can be "tamed" and taught to perform on command such as birds and circus animals. While tame and approachable, they still maintain the unpredictable factor. These animals by no means take great comfort in being where they are. Many have grown used to their life and would not survive in the wild, but their DNA is not programmed to live a life such as they do. They are tolerant of human interaction. While they may be grateful for seeing their trainer, and develop a relationship with them, it is still not natural to them. This would even include the ones born in captivity that become "pets," such as reptiles, rodents, and fish.

There is a gray line between a tame and domesticated animal, as Thuriel shares. Tame animals are reliant on humans for their well-being and survival, just like domesticated pets. However, the biggest difference between the two is as follows: the tamed animal does not thrive on human interaction, while domesticated animals do. As a member of your family, a true bond of love is formed, a companionship between you and your domesticated pet that gives you both great joy. One gets excited to see the other, playtime ensues, you search for that perfect toy, food, or doctor to show your love for them. You engage throughout your day to interact with them. Gabi, our yogi doodle dog, and I engage in daily downward dog poses; it's something she does naturally and is one of the many ways we share a moment.

Thuriel can be instrumental in strengthening your connection to your totem animal as well. If this is a new term for you, allow me to explain. A totem is a being, object, or symbol represented by an animal or plant that serves as an emblem of a group of people, such as a family, clan, group, lineage, or tribe, reminding them of their ancestry. A totem animal can also be a symbol of a specific goal or energy.

As an example, a dove is universally accepted as a symbol of peace. A lion stands for courage and pride. A cat is associated with independence. Dogs symbolize loyalty. Get the idea? What other animals can you think of that stand for a specific energy?

There are many phrases that revolve around a specific animal, such as "sly as a fox" or "an elephant never forgets." See how integrated animal energy is within our life? Isn't it time to better understand and learn from them? Chat with Thuriel.

Your totem animal is one that was assigned or chosen at your birth via a soul contract. Your totem animal tends to shift with each life, unlike your guardian angel who is constant in every life. Your totem animal is representative of your mission in this life and holds the qualities that you exude or wish to exude. Remember, most don't remember what their mission is, what life lessons are agreed to be experienced, etc. However, discovering your totem animal can offer deep insights into who you are; not only at a soul level, but into your life's mission. One of my totem animals is the unicorn. Yes, you read that correctly. While this animal may be considered mythical, it still holds within it great power and one that I treasure.

As life ebbs and flows, other animals come in and out to support you depending on the cycle of your life, what you are working through, on, toward, etc.; much like the various angels that float in and out depending on what life adventure you are experiencing. The animal totems frequently make themselves known in a variety of ways: commercials, dreams, physical in your life, etc. As an example, when we lived in Maryland, I kept seeing elephants. Elephants! They showed up on TV commercials, billboards even began popping up in my daydreams. It was so obvious, it became a joke within the family. Off I went to chat with elephant and its meaning and message for me. All was given and spot on for that moment in time. Once received, I stopped seeing them. As you go about your day, notice what animals catch your eye. It doesn't have to be one that you feel drawn to, but one that is seemingly everywhere you are.

This also applies to animals you are fearful of. Spiders? Dogs? Cats? Look up their meaning and you will learn something else about yourself that is perhaps waiting to be better acknowledged from within. Better yet, chat with Thuriel to gather insights that are specific to you and your question!

Thuriel's Name Defined

Simply put, Thuriel's name is loosely defined as angel of the animals. He has under his jurisdiction the entire animal kingdom: domesticated, wild, reptilian, aviary, equine, mammals, aquatic, etc.

Angelic Encounter

I have shared the elephant connection already, but another angelic encounter that revolved around Thuriel is as follows: I had been working and chatting with Thuriel longer than I realized, for one day I was sitting with Gabi and our two cats, Linus and Schroeder, and I realized we were having a full-blown conversation!

Schroder the cat is the alpha of the group. This always amuses me since Gabi is a good four times the size of him. Schroeder rules, others drool, as far as he is concerned. We were cuddling, as we had just returned from another road trip for my business, Angel Chatter, and we were catching up on their excursions while at home or at the "spa" (my term to ease the guilt of putting Gabi periodically in the kennel). Who did she play with? Why were the two cats still afraid of the teenage girl coming in daily (for three years, mind you) to tend to them and hopefully play with them?

It was fascinating!

If you have a pet, I highly recommend a regular chat with them. You will be amazed at what you learn.

Thuriel's Light Temple

Thuriel's light temple is located in Australia. When I asked him about this, the answer was quick and decisive—where else can you find such an unusual collection of animals that still walk the earth? Indeed, Thuriel, indeed!

Thuriel's Symbol

Look at Thuriel's symbol—does it remind you of an animal figure? Perhaps one similar to what could be drawn in prehistoric cave dwellings? It starts high this time, allowing you to reach up into an animal's energy to receive their messages. Why high? Animals are not bogged down with egos and the fear that runs amuck with us humans. Their energy and their mission is often a simple but powerful reminder to live in the moment.

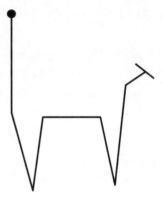

As you gaze upon Thuriel's symbol, it seems to dillydally around to create the animal image. Energetically it is actually grounding these messages into your psyche to help you better understand and integrate their messages, enabling you to pass along whatever it is they wish to share.

Thuriel's Compass Direction

You are most likely not surprised that Thuriel is not associated with a compass direction. As the overseer of the entire animal kingdom, animals are worldwide: north, south, east, and west. Thuriel is forever by their side helping them as the other gang members help us, the humans.

Thuriel's Chakra Association

As you have most likely suspected, Thuriel is not associated with any chakra. Why would he be? He oversees the animal kingdom, so, very much like Metatron, he could oversee the entire chakra system. Doesn't one feel great love when snuggling their fur baby? Doesn't one quiet their mind when their pet is nearby? One may feel more protected when they are walking with you or home alone with you. One may even feel more creative when their muse is hanging out with them. The list goes on and on and on, as animals connect to our chakra system.

Angelic Activity

This activity is geared more toward the pet owner; however, anyone can do this while out and about in nature, at a zoo, pet farm, working farm, basically anywhere there are animals!

As you sit quietly, gaze upon the animal and ask if they have a message for you.
You may wish to place your hands over your heart to help quiet the mind.
Breathe more slowly to disengage from the what's-acceptable syndrome.
Ask your question again.

Listen with your heart. Write down your answers. Then, feel free to analyze. Some of the messages may be very general and direct. Keep in mind, like any new tool, the more comfortable you get with it, the deeper the messages will become.

Thuriel's Healing Crystal

Thuriel's crystal choice is rainforest jasper. This crystal is known for imbuing soft gradual energies, and can contribute to more cheerful and pleasant people entering your life. It is chosen for Thuriel due to its equally strong energetic connection to healing in connection with the earth, plants, trees, and of course, animals. Rainforest jasper exudes a vibration of happiness and joy for life that flows outward throughout your life. Isn't that what all animals are ultimately trying to teach us? Live life in the moment of now?

Rainforest jasper also carries a strong vibration for change. How do you wish to be the change in the world? How can you be of service? Another added plus for rainforest jasper: it also opens the communicative door between you and the devic world (faeries, mermaids, etc.).

Angelic Aromatherapy

Thuriel connects with animals and nature, right? Is it any surprise that his most favorite scents are wrapped up in **fir needle**, **cypress**, **pine**, and **oak moss**? Each one of these scents heralds in the great outdoors and infuses that gentle reminder that we are one with nature and animals. They inspire you to reconnect with them. Weather not conducive? Sit by a window and let your eyes wander. Weather conducive? Find the time to connect. The world is much bigger than is realized, and when you are out and about in it, it can be a healing balm for the soul.

Thuriel's Askfirmations

Why is it so easy for me to understand my pet's needs/worries/thoughts?
Why is it so easy for me to chat and understand animals?
Why is it so easy for me to embrace the lessons that animals teach?

Guided Meditation with Archangel Thuriel

Sit facing any direction.

Breathe in for four counts,
Hold for four counts,
Breathe out for four counts.

Call on Archangel Michael and his legions,
To stand guard while you meditate.

Breathe in for four counts,
Hold for four counts,
Breathe out for four counts.

The room fills.
It gets warmer,
As Michael and his legion enter to stand guard,
During this meditation.

Breathe in for four counts,
Hold for four counts,
Breathe out for four counts.

It is now time to call on,
Archangel Thuriel and your totem animal.

As they enter,
Your vision begins to shift from viewing the room,
In which you sit,
To the great outdoors.

Breathe in for four counts,
Hold for four counts,
Breathe out for four counts.

With each breath,
Your view of the great outdoors,
Continues to expand.

Breathe in for four counts,
Hold for four counts,
Breathe out for four counts.

With each breath,
Your view of the great outdoors,
Becomes more defined.

Breathe in for four counts,
Hold for four counts,
Breathe out for four counts.

With each breath,
Thuriel steps closer,
And brings with him,
Your totem animal.

Breathe in for four counts,
Hold for four counts,
Breathe out for four counts.

As they approach,
You smile.

Breathe in for four counts,
Hold for four counts,
Breathe out for four counts.

As they approach,
Your heart expands.

Breathe in for four counts,
Hold for four counts,
Breathe out for four counts.

With each step, they get closer.
With each breath,
They are nearer.

Breathe in for four counts,
Hold for four counts,
Breathe out for four counts.

They are finally in front of you.

Breathe in for four counts,
Hold for four counts,
Breathe out for four counts.

Thuriel reaches for your hand.

Breathe in for four counts,
Hold for four counts,
Breathe out for four counts.

As you touch,
He brings your hand gently,
To the face of your totem animal.

Breathe in for four counts,
Hold for four counts,
Breathe out for four counts.

As your hand caresses,
Its face,
It looks into your eyes.

Breathe in for four counts,
Hold for four counts,
Breathe out for four counts.

There is a heart-to-heart connection.

Breathe in for four counts,
Hold for four counts,
Breathe out for four counts.

As your hand lingers,
It gently moves its head in order to lick your hand.

Breathe in for four counts,
Hold for four counts,
Breathe out for four counts.

Your totem animal brings with it great power,
Power that helps you move through life,
With grace, love, joy, and power.

Breathe in for four counts,
Hold for four counts,
Breathe out for four counts.

Its presence now is this reminder.

Breathe in for four counts,
Hold for four counts,
Breathe out for four counts.

Repeat.

Breathe in for four counts,
Hold for four counts,
Breathe out for four counts.

Your totem animal now speaks to your heart,
Relaying a message that will infuse into your soul.

Breathe in for four counts,
Hold for four counts,
Breathe out for four counts.

As their message sinks in,
You are reminded that you may call upon them,
Whenever you require that boost, that shot of animal energy,
To catapult you to the next level,
Or to simply get through the day.

Breathe in for four counts,
Hold for four counts,
Breathe out for four counts.

You release your hand from their face.

Breathe in for four counts,
Hold for four counts,
Breathe out for four counts.

As the connection is slowly diminishing,
The view begins to fade.

Breathe in for four counts,
Hold for four counts,
Breathe out for four counts.

With each breath, the definition of your surroundings becomes,
More watery in view.

Breathe in for four counts,
Hold for four counts,
Breathe out for four counts.

With each breath,
You become more aware of your surroundings,
In the present.

Breathe in for four counts,
Hold for four counts,
Breathe out for four counts.

You feel your body once more.

Breathe in for four counts,
Hold for four counts,
Breathe out for four counts.

You wiggle your toes and hands.

Breathe in for four counts,
Hold for four counts,
Breathe out for four counts.

You slowly open your eyes.

Breathe in for four counts,
Hold for four counts,
Breathe out for four counts.

You inhale deeply and exhale loudly.
Welcome back.

15

Guardian Angel
(Your Bestie)

"Dearest, I am with you always. I always have been, I always will be. Just ask and I am there."

—Your Guardian Angel (aka bestie with wings)

Your guardian angel has been with you since the very first time you were born. They are your best friend to help you find a parking spot, perfect job, home, mate, and so much more. My clients often ask how to know what their guardian angel's name is. Honestly, whatever name comes to you first. It can be angelic sounding, such as Michael, Tzaphiel, or Azrael, or it can be Bob, Steve, Lisa, or Gertrude. It truly doesn't matter what name you assign to your angel. It's your relationship with your best friend; therefore, what name would you give your best friend?

Your guardian angel has been with you since the first time you incarnated. Every single life. They know more about you than you ever will. They know the great and not so great things about you. They know you are human and therefore gloriously imperfect.

Your Guardian Angel's Name Defined

As you know by now, Raphael oversees all the guardian angels. As so many wish for a name to connect with, start with him if you are unsure of your guardian angel's name. Ask that Raphael reintroduce you both. Keep in mind that your guardian angel's name will reflect your relationship with them. As mentioned above, don't get caught up in your angel's name. Don't be surprised if it turns out that Toby is your guardian angel's name, or Michael or Grace or Gabe or . . . well, you catch my drift. Your guardian angel doesn't change from life to life, but since you change, their name may change to better assimilate into your life now.

You may simply ask, "What is your name?" Be still for a moment or two. A name typically pops into your head within those moments. How does it feel to you? Does it make you smile? Giggle? Those are two great signs that you are spot on. If their name still eludes you, chat with Raphael. This is an especially powerful exercise/request to do upon retiring for the evening. Ask as you curl up in bed. Many clients wake up with a name running through their head in the morning. How easy is that?

Angelic Encounter

I've already shared my "Pinky!" story with you earlier (p. ix), so I won't duplicate it. However, there is not a single day goes by that Pinky and I aren't chatting about something. Some days our conversations are definitely more on the mundane side: while at a private pet store that I adore, I was reaching for a bag of cat litter when Pinky popped in and told me, *no*, go to one of the big box stores. Okaaay . . . weird . . . but okaaay. As the big box store was on my way home, it wasn't a big deal. To my surprise, when I got to the cat litter area, not only was my brand on sale, but there was a damaged bag at an even lower price than the sale! I saved about fifteen dollars on the bag! Thanks, Ariel!

Of course, our conversations can go rather deep, as well. These typically happen when Gabi and I are out for our daily hike and I've set an intention before I step a foot out the door. On those days, a wide variety of things will catch my eye and seemingly random thoughts pop in that when I connect the dots, my next course of action becomes crystal clear.

Your Guardian Angel's Light Temple

As you have probably guessed, there is no specific light temple for your guardian angel. You may of course use Raphael's, which is Fátima. However, the very best place for your guardian angel's light temple is within you. Your heart. Your heart is all; it is the birthplace of your soul, and what better location for your guardian angel to reside?

Your Guardian Angel's Symbol

This is indeed a very personal decision; perhaps more personal than their name. What design, symbol, sigil would you create that represents your guardian angel? Not sure? Set your intention and begin doodling. Within that doodle is great power. Within that doodle is their sigil—no longer a doodle, but a sign that strengthens your connection to them.

Your Guardian Angel's Compass Direction

You are beginning to see the theme here of no right or wrong answer in this chapter. That theme continues. As your guardian angel is always with you, there is no wrong direction to have a more powerful chat. There is no right direction to make it more empowering. The answers are all within you.

Your Guardian Angel's Chakra Association

The theme continues once more of no true answer. Every bit of you is precious. Every bit of you is powerful. Every bit of you is important. Therefore, every bit of you, every chakra within and beyond you connects with your guardian angel.

Angelic Activity

I've alluded to a couple of things you can do within this chapter:

- ★ Set your intention prior to an outing. Your intention can be getting clarity on a particular event, relationship, or the next step you are muddled about. It is best to do this one when you will be by yourself. It will allow you to overhear chance conversations if you are out doing errands or vegging at your local coffee shop, bistro, etc. It will be easier to spy the various signs that your guardian angel will arrange to provide answers and to become inspired for that next step if you are alone. It is rather easy to get caught up in conversations with another; allowing the conversation to flow, respond, act, react, etc., but because your attention is elsewhere, the signs won't always be readily seen.

★ Ask and receive! You may initially start with the unveiling-of-their-name-while-sleeping ritual, but asking and receiving is also another valuable tool to use for any situation. Wish better clarity with a magic wand? Ask, just once, as you prepare for bed. Ask with sincerity, not sarcastic wit, and let the energy that is wrapped up around it float away. Sounds a bit easier to do than it is at times, so read a good book, meditate, make love, doodle, etc. Anything to get your mind off the issue at hand. You have placed your intention that you will receive the answers while you sleep and retain them upon awakening. The angels hear and obey, so all you must do is allow.

Your Guardian Angel's Crystal

My favorite universal crystal for working with the guardian angels is celestite, sought after for its very high energetic frequencies and sublime divine energies. Sound convoluted? Hardly. This gentle energy stone is extremely powerful, but like many others suggested throughout the book, very gentle. This may be your forever guardian angel crystal, but you may also use this one initially to strengthen your connection with your angelic BFF.

Once your relationship becomes more real to you, your crystal choice may change to better reflect your journey in this life. For example, the crystal I have sought for years is tiger eye, from science museum field trips in elementary school (I was the first one to dive into the crystal bin and come up with as many tiger eye crystals as possible) to now incorporating it into my jewelry designs. Why so much tiger eye? For me, it offers organizational skills (something I desperately can use at times when I get in high creative mode). It enhances or solidifies my little-miss-know-it-all capabilities. In other words, I've learned to trust those inklings better, thanks to that stone. Lastly, I LOVE the way it looks!

Your Guardian Angel's Aromatherapy

Much like your guardian angel's crystal, the scent of choice will vary from person to person. For some reason, the scent of chocolate chip cookies may repel some folks (heresy, I know), so how could that enhance their relationship with their guardian angel if that scent repels them? It can't, obviously.

What are some of your favorite scents? Why? Explore each one. Do they harken to childhood? Those most likely are not your guardian angel's scent. Does it expand the soul, make you smile, and overall feel uplifted? That most likely is your scent to connect with your guardian angel.

Mine? Jasmine mixed with a bit of rose.

Your Guardian Angel's Askfirmations

Why it is so easy to chat and hear my guardian angel?
Why is it so easy to know my guardian angel's name?
Why do I feel worthy to have a guardian angel?

Meditation to Reconnect with Your Guardian Angel

Call on Archangel Michael,

Breathe in,
Hold for four counts,
Breathe out.

Feel the room become more sacred,
As Michael and his legions join you in your sacred space.

As they continue to file in the room, you relax.

Breathe in,
Hold for four counts,
Breathe out.

Your heart beats slower in love and peace.

Breathe in,
Hold for four counts,
Breathe out.

You ask for Raphael's assistance,
To connect more clearly with your guardian angel.

Breathe in,
Hold for four counts,
Breathe out.

As Raphael enters and you continue to relax,
You see before you a beautiful vista.

It has all that you adore,
The perfect amount of sun,
Just the right breeze,
A gentle brook rambling nearby.

The birds twitter in anticipation of your arrival.
Your favorite flowers are in bloom,
And gently scent your path.

Your path is clear.
You continue to walk,
And come upon a secluded glen.

Angels encircle the glen as a form of protective love.
This is your sacred place.
Nobody enters unless you request.

You may ask that all angels continue to guard your glen,
To give you peace of mind that it stays sacred.

Within the glen is a spot for you to sit upon.
It conforms beautifully to your body,
And offers the perfect support.

The breeze caresses your face,
The sun warms your skin.
As you sit in total peace and relaxation,
A being is noticed on the horizon.

It approaches.
As they come closer,
You recognize them!

The coloring of their garments,
Their hair,
How they move,
All is as it was before, in perfect harmony.

As they come before you, they, too, sit down.
You gently hold hands.
Oh, the comfort and love that transcends into your body.

You remember.

Breathe in,
Hold for four counts,
Breathe out.

Memories of time spent together in various lives,
Come back.

Breathe in,
Hold for four counts,
Breathe out.

Your best friend has returned.
Actually, they remind you they have never left;
You just forgot.

You both begin to talk,
To share,
To remember,
To ask,
To answer.

Breathe in,
Hold for four counts,
Breathe out.

Breathe in,
Hold for four counts,
Breathe out.

Breathe in,
Hold for four counts,
Breathe out.

Breathe in,
Hold for four counts,
Breathe out.

You feel full.
You ask one final question for today.

What is their name?

Breathe in,
Hold for four counts,
Breathe out.

They hold your face in their hands and tell you.

Breathe in,
Hold for four counts,
Breathe out.

They remind you that they are always here for you,
All you need to do is ask.

Breathe in,
Hold for four counts,
Breathe out.

You both rise and know it is time to end today's conversation.

As you part, you are once again reminded,
That you may come here,
Any day,
At any time.

It is your space.

Breathe in,
Hold for four counts,
Breathe out.

As you count backward from ten to one,
You become more alert,
More aware of the sounds in your space,
The furnishings in your room,
Your breathing.

You gently move your fingers and toes,
You breathe in deeply,
Exhale loudly.

Your eyes open.
The world is fresh and new once more,
For you remember,
You are loved always,
And in all ways.

16

Angelic Signs

This book could go on forever, but in an effort not to dawdle, it's time to wrap everything up in angelic wings. The angels are always giving us signs that they are with us. The easiest way to see them? Allow yourself to receive. It really is that simple. Open your beautiful eyes to the world around you and tell them that you are ready. I frequently chat with them on my daily walk, and before I get home from that same walk, I've received insights from many sources: nature, songs, thoughts, a chance meeting with a new friend. Of course, these messages are all from the angels and ultimately answer the question I posed prior to leaving our home.

Remember, the word *angel* translates to mean "messenger of God." They hear the prayers, soul yearnings, and lovingly leave calling cards of their presence. They deliver the message; my only question is this, *are you listening?*

The signs the angels leave us are as bountiful as a fall harvest. Really. Following are some ways that are more traditional and will hopefully prompt you to become even more observant with your life and enhance your connection with the angels.

Have you ever been walking down the street, in your own home, or at your place of employment and found a white feather? This is one of their more infamous calling cards. In fact, years ago, I participated in a ceremony and upon leaving, a friend noticed two small white feathers fanned out along my spinal column! I think my wings sprouted for all to see that evening and haven't stopped growing since.

Finding a white feather in unusual places is a true eye-grabber. Who wouldn't notice a white feather in the middle of a parking lot, or even inside your home?

When you do find one, and you will, give thanks for the confirmation of their presence in your life. Next, hold the feather close to your heart and ask what message the angels wish to convey to you. Why your heart? It's the birthplace of your soul, and what better place to receive a message from the angels? The message may or may not be crystal clear, but you will be inspired to take action on something. The action could be to take a nap because you have overtaxed yourself. The message could be that you are loved. It could be offering insight into something you have been grappling with for a bit. It's as endless as the universe is large. In fact, as I was typing up this chapter, I glanced out my office window and saw two white feathers floating upward! Talk about unusual!

Of course, there are more than just white feathers out there. The following chart offers other ideas for the various colored feathers you may find. Is a color not listed? Chat with Thuriel and Raziel to discover its meaning for you!

	Feather Colors and Their Symbolic Meanings
Blue	Protection, mental abilities, communication, peace, and intuitive abilities
Black	Mystical wisdom, protection, initiation
Brown	Grounding
Gray	Peace
Green	Harmony, prosperity, money, health, nature spirits, healing
Orange	Energy, creativity, success, playfulness
Pink	Self-love, romance, kindness
Purple	Spirituality, higher consciousness
White	Purity, hope, peace, moon
Yellow	Youth, power, sun, mental agility

Another great angel nudge is the number four. It has long been associated with the angelic realm. There is power in multiples, such as the time of 4:44. However, why limit to only seeing this combination? What if you saw only a single four; does that mean they aren't *really* with you? Of course not! Remember, it's only a sign and how you interpret it.

They may actually *chat* with you! Not inner hearing, but a true, audible voice. This tends to be on the rarer side, but can and does happen in order for you to pay attention immediately. The angels may also appear in physical form. Angels take human form to assist us out of a dangerous moment, or to pass along information in a moment of need. Have you ever met a stranger who seemingly appeared out of nowhere to assist you along the way? Thank the angels. I've even had total strangers approach me in department stores and suggest I try on a new style of clothing. Initially, I took it to be polite. They stayed in the store (eventually, I started keeping watch, wanting to make sure they were, well, human) while I would pop in the dressing room and change very quickly. Sometimes, I would emerge from the store and they were nowhere to be seen. It's happened more than once.

However, my all-time favorite angelic story is as follows: My honey and I had gone on a second honeymoon while my parents watched our daughters. My dad returned home for business reasons a few days prior to us returning. At the time, they lived close to twelve hours away. Almost immediately, he began to suffer some chest pains. My mom quickly arranged child care for the last thirty-six hours with our dear friends and neighbors and rushed to her love's side (all turned out well and they are both still very much here and in love). Of course, all of this happened unbeknownst to us as we were out of cell phone range.

As our boat pulled into port, we received the messages. Of course, we knew the girls were fine, but there was now a sense of urgency on our part to get home. I told "The Gang" I wanted to be home *now*! Mama bear wanted to hug her cubs! Once we cleared customs, we raced and found a cab who promptly took us to the train station. Well, promptly is a choice term, traffic was traffic—slow. I got antsy. Couldn't even sit still in the cab. We knew that according to the train schedule, one was leaving within the hour and the other not until several hours later. Guess which one I was going for? You got it, the first. The second wasn't an option for me, and I conveyed that to them in no uncertain terms.

Upon arriving at the train station, cars were parked two or three deep from the curb. We began to do a little panic dance. Okay, I increased the antsy factor. We hopped out of the car, grabbed our suitcases, and as I turned around a redcap appeared to help us with the luggage.

He inquired if we needed assistance. *Yes*! I explained our situation, and he replied, "No problem, ma'am." He calmly piled everything up on his cart and escorted us to the counter to purchase our tickets for the next train. Not a person was ahead of us! He sauntered over to the escalator, smiled, and waved while we purchased the tickets. Tickets in hand, we ran back to him and down the escalator we three traveled. He then tucked us into our car and placed the luggage on the shelving overhead. As we turned to give him a huge tip, he was gone. We were the only ones on the train at that point. I even ventured out of the car, and the platform was empty! He was truly nowhere to be found.

You tell me, human or angel?

I choose angel. He appeared to us in a moment of need, took care of the entire situation, and vanished. Think back to your own life; how many times has something similar happened to you?

Angels can also leave a whiff of heavenly aroma in their wake. There have been a few times when I have had the pleasure of smelling roses when there are no roses in the house. Jasmine is one of my favorite angelic scents, and I've been blessed to smell this on occasion, as well, with no jasmine for miles. The angels simply wanted me to be sure that I knew they were close, as always.

Another angelic tactic is wind. We have all been outside on a windy day. However, have you ever been outside when the air is still and a soft breeze flows through or near you? That is an angel lovingly letting their presence in your life be known.

Numbers are a glorious way in which the angels convey messages. Each number conveys a different message. If this tactic intrigues you, search the Internet and find a source that resonates best with you.

In closing, remember that the angels are always with you, acknowledged or not. Angels always respond to every request. It is up to us to allow the true message to come through, for it always does, just not in the manner we may expect!

Lastly, remember, now and forever more,

You are worthy of all you desire.
You are worthy of living life on your terms.
You are a magnificent being.

Glossary of Terms

Angel Symbols

I channeled the symbols in this book several years ago in one evening. Each symbol has three things in common: the starting point (circle/dot), ending point (line), and all can be drawn in one motion. Each symbol is angelic language that will strengthen your connection to that particular angel. As there are many languages across the earth, there are many languages of the angels. This is one of them.

Askfirmations

Simply defined, an askfirmation is an affirmation in the form of a question. The universe answers every question literally. The universe does not interpret. All askfirmations you do ask are lovingly responded to by the universe, angels included. The answers come in subtle yet profound ways. The way the message is conveyed is as varied and unique as each person. Yes, there's a book for that (*Askfirmations*).

Chakra

The word *chakra* is translated from Sanskrit to mean wheel. A chakra is an energy vortex within your body that oversees certain bodily and spiritual functions. The ones widely recognized align with the spinal column, but there are many outside the body such as earth star and soul star.

Ley Lines

You may be familiar with the longitude and latitude, the lines that cover the earth and help with geographic locations. Ley lines are similar in that they are also straight, but can also go in a diagonal line. Because of this feature, many lines can meet at one point, creating a vortex of energy that creates its unique thumbprint known for healing, spiritual advancement, astral travel, etc.

Light Temple

A light temple is an energetic temple. You will not go to any light temple location and find a physical building dedicated to that angel. It is where the ley lines (see above definition) converge to create a strong energy center that connects with a certain angel, ascended master, etc.

Orbs

An orb is often captured on film. However, don't confuse them with lens refractions that can also be seen on film. Typically, one will see many orbs on their photos during times of high importance: graduation, weddings, funerals (although let's face it, we don't take many photos during times of stress), school gatherings, sports, plays, concerts, etc. When they appear in your photos, you have captured an energy! They are angels, but could also be a departed loved one, making their presence known.